Library of
Davidson College

Aspects of Political Theory
Classical Concepts in an Age of Relativism

Works by W J Stankiewicz

Books

Institutional Changes in the Postwar Economy of Poland (with J M Montias) (1955)
Politics & Religion in 17th-Century France (1960)
Canada–US Relations & Canadian Foreign Policy (1973)
Aspects of Political Theory: Classical Concepts in an Age of Relativism (1976)

Anthologies and Symposia

Political Thought Since World War II: Critical & Interpretive Essays (1964)
Crisis in British Government: the Need for Reform (1967)
In Defense of Sovereignty (1969)
British Government in an Era of Reform (1976)

Essays, Aphorisms and Other

The Living Name (1964)
What is Behavioralism? Thoughts on the Crisis in the Social Sciences (1971)
Relativism: Thoughts & Aphorisms (1972)
A Guide to Democratic Jargon (1976)

Aspects of Political Theory

Classical Concepts in an Age of Relativism

W J Stankiewicz
Professor of Political Science
University of British Columbia

Collier Macmillan
London

A Collier Macmillan book, published by
CASSELL & COLLIER MACMILLAN PUBLISHERS LTD
35 Red Lion Square, London WC1R 4SG
Sydney, Auckland, Toronto, Johannesburg

An affiliate of Macmillan Publishing Co Inc,
New York

Copyright © W J Stankiewicz, 1976

All rights reserved. No part of this publication may be reproduced,
stored in a retrieval system, or transmitted, in any form or by
any means, electronic, mechanical, photocopying, recording or otherwise,
without the prior permission in writing of the Publishers

First published 1976

ISBN 0 02 977630 9

Filmset in 'Monophoto' Baskerville 11 on 12½ pt by
Richard Clay (The Chaucer Press), Ltd, Bungay, Suffolk
and printed in Great Britain by
Fletcher & Son Ltd, Norwich

To Marketa

Preface

I am much indebted to my friends, Mr Ian W Peyman and Mr Ronald C Cooke, for their co-operation and advice; to my academic colleagues Professors D C Corbett, Maurice Cranston, F H Hinsley, Anthony Parel, Albert Shalom and Dr June Gow for reading the manuscript (or parts of it) and offering criticism and suggestions; and to my wife, Dr Marketa Goetz Stankiewicz, for her help and assistance in the preparation of this book.

I am grateful to Dr Walter H Gage, past President of the University of British Columbia, for his encouragement; to the University Committee on Research at UBC for financial assistance; and to the Canada Council and the Isaak Walton Killam Memorial Fund for the grant of a Leave Fellowship and a Senior Killam Fellowship respectively.

I am also indebted to the responsive audiences of universities which were exposed to some of the ideas developed in this book: in Europe, at the London School of Economics and Political Science, St John's College (Cambridge), and the University of Stockholm; in Canada, at the University of Toronto, Queen's University, and the University of Victoria; in New Zealand, at the University of Auckland, Victoria University of Wellington, and the University of Otago; in Australia, at the following universities: Sydney, New South Wales, Queensland, Melbourne, La Trobe, Flinders, Adelaide, and the Australian National University.

A section of Chapter III of this book served as the basis for a paper 'Sovereign Authority and the Function of Law in a Democratic Society', which was prepared for the World Congress on Philosophy of Law and Social Philosophy,

Madrid, 7–12 September 1973, and published in *Anuario de Filosofia del Derecho* (1973–74); part of Chapter I appeared in *Political Science* (Wellington) (December 1974); Chapter IV in *Political Studies* (June 1976); and part of Chapter VII in *Contemporary Review* (September 1976).

                W J STANKIEWICZ
                University of British Columbia
                July 1976

Contents

Preface	vii
Introduction	1
I Is the Social Contract Obsolete?	7
Individualist Values v Social Order	8
Individualism, the Social Contract and Constitutionalism	11
Contractualism v Relativism and Individualism v Egalitarianism	15
Obligation and Consent in the Social Contract	19
Contractual and Representative Views of Government and the 'Prisoner's Dilemma'	21
Uses of the 'Prisoner's Dilemma'	24
II The General Will and the Public Interest	25
Transformation of the General Will	25
The General Will and Totalitarianism	27
The General Will and Democracy	30
Public Interest	33
Public Interest and a 'Mythologized' Rousseau	37
Public Interest Norms and the Democratic Order	41
The Content of Public Interest	43
III Sovereignty and the Crisis of Authority	47
The Crisis of Authority	47
Authority, Freedom and Rule-Governed Activities	54

Authority and Political Obligation	59
Sovereign Authority and Sovereign Law	61
Is 'Authority' a Substitute for 'Sovereignty'?	66

IV Sovereignty in Political Theory   69

The Nature of Sovereignty	69
A Re-Wording of the Classical Definition of Sovereignty	75
The Significance of Sovereignty	77
Sovereignty and the Public Interest	79
Sovereignty as a Tool of Analysis	82
Legitimacy and Sovereignty	87
Sovereignty as a Datum in International Relations	90
The Exercise of Sovereignty and Relativism	94

V Natural Law   96

'A Peculiar Tone of Horror'	96
The Persistence of Natural Law	99
Relativism, Reason and Natural Law	100
'Relative' Natural Law	103
Who Shall Determine Natural Law and How?	104
Positive and Natural Law and Ideology	109

VI From Natural Law to Public Philosophy   114

'Applied' Natural Law in Democratic Societies	114
Obligation and Two Sets of Societal Norms	117
Ethical Considerations in Positive Law	119

The Problem of Democracy and 'Natural Law'	123
Public Philosophy	125

VII The Consequences of Relativism and Behaviouralism — 128

The Essence of Modern Relativism	129
Relativism and the Springs of Action: Norms as Tools of Analysis	131
Relativism as a Methodology	133
Relativity and Relativism	135
Relativism and Political Science	137
Relativism and the Hierarchy of Values	139
The Consequences of Scientism	144
Is an 'Empirically-Based Theory' Possible?	147
Computer-Made Theory, Experimental Ideologies and 'Instant' Systems	153
Can Philosophy and Science be Reconciled?	155
The Consequences of Behaviouralism	158
Is Post-Behaviouralism Possible?	161
Normativism, Relevance and Rationalism	163
Post-script: Spragens' Postbehavioural Dilemma	166

Index — 171

Introduction

The present work continues an endeavour whose immediate aim is to reconstruct some 'classical' concepts of political theory and fit them into a present-day setting; or, in other words, traditional concepts are used as a basis for the discussion of contemporary political predicaments. The endeavour began with the publication of the symposium *In Defense of Sovereignty* (Oxford University Press, New York, 1969) and will extend beyond the present volume. Its long-range goal is to consider under a common denominator—RELATIVISM IN POLITICS—various aspects of theory such as the basic concepts discussed in the present essay, together with modern theories of democracy and the wider spectrum of political ideologies to be discussed in subsequent volumes.

What rules must be followed in an enterprise of this sort? It must not be a chronicle of the great philosophers' legacy, a catalogue of their theories, a structure erected on quotable statements from contemporary scholars, nor an exercise in typology. It has to eschew sociological 'scientism' (which results in model-building and abstract theorizing). It must combine some of the tasks of an historian, such as preserving what is valuable in philosophic tradition, with those of a philosopher—linking that which is worth preserving with the present and projecting it into the future (by distilling and transcending contemporary experience). It must not only rescue certain concepts from oblivion but analyse others—their derivatives—whose present significance has not been made evident. It must reveal the important issues arising within the field: questions posed by the classical thinkers who invented the terms; the ideological framework of values within which the latter must be discussed; current ways of thinking about the democratic system; the consequences of introspection and self-awareness induced by modern political science. It is with the subject matter lying between these broad limits that the present study is concerned.

Some years ago I realized that relativism—the leading theme of the present work—is one of the most striking characteristics of our society. While analysing its impact on political theory, I have endeavoured to avoid the conceptual tangle of its many 'types' and hence, for the most part, their categorization and definition. Instead, I have tried to reveal the all-pervasive nature and 'essence' of relativism. I have also avoided dwelling on the particular arguments advanced by various 'schools' of relativism, since I have come to the conclusion that they all combine to make a case for relativism. I assumed the latter to be a belief regarding norms—a belief which became a philosophical system. As such, the notion not only provided me with a focus for the various concepts of political theory with which I was directly concerned but made me see contemporary life in the light of this widely diffused philosophy.

In an essay on contemporary political theory one is bound to ask two questions: How justified is the claim of the 'revival' of theory (only two decades after a 'demise' of political theory was proclaimed) and what are its prospects?

Unless there is a change in the attitude of non-theorists toward theory, and behaviouralists and others feel that theory's claims are legitimate, there is no point in talking about a 'revival' of theory. Regardless of how much theorizing there is, theory cannot be said to have revived until its relation to empirical studies has been accepted by both theorists and empiricists.

Political theory itself has, of course, never been opposed. What, however, until recently had been steadily losing ground is the traditional method of combining theorizing through normative analysis with practical observation. Before the rise of scientific methodology this was the only method of analysing political behaviour. As science developed rigorous techniques of evidence, political theorizing in the classical tradition appeared unmethodical, dangerously speculative and tainted with normative apologetics. If what was wanted was a political *science*, there seemed no place for political theory, except as it developed from the new methodology.

But this attitude has recently been changing. Firstly, analysis of the relationship between empirical observations and scientific statements has made it apparent that it is not illegitimate to analyse data in terms of a theory that in time preceded the observations which it professes to describe. Indeed, it may well be that there is no other way of conducting meaningful empirical observations. Secondly, and even more important, increasing doubts have arisen about 'scientism'—the supposition that all phenomena must be amenable to the empirical method. Human behaviour, which seems to fit the categories 'purposeful' and 'elective' rather than 'caused' and 'determined', appears now unsuited to analysis by traditional scientific methodology. The approach of the theorists—which in the early days of scientific method seemed outmoded—can now be seen to have as much claim to legitimacy as the strict empiricist approach. Today, outright rejection of theory is no longer typical of most political scientists. This may lead to what I have elsewhere called a 'secondary iconoclasm'.

Yet a change in attitude towards what one might call the legitimacy of theorizing cannot itself be called a revival of political theory. What can be easily mistaken for such a revival is the presentation of second-hand accounts of great theorists. For instance, the point that needs to be made about Hobbes's theory of sovereignty is not that, in essence, he said this and that. True revival comes only when we understand that there may be a meaningful relationship between the theory he evolved at a special moment in history and our own particular moment in history. This is the difference between the approach of the theorist and that of the empiricist. The theorist believes that a significant theory does not relate only to a special moment in history, though in its formulation it must have been influenced by special circumstances. It never describes the circumstances as purely empirical analyses do. If it has any merit at all, it says something enduring about society. It says something of lasting value because the norms it manipulates endure, even though all else changes.

Thus Hobbes—who wished he lived under an absolutist monarchy (he in fact lived under competing absolutisms)—analysed the relations between government and society in terms of the norms of law and security. If we consider his analysis only in relation to this period and seek only to discover what he 'really' said, we commit the error made by many political theorists in the past: we suppose that the most significant factor behind Hobbes' theory is the fact that he lived under an absolutist monarchy and that his formulation is for our purposes irremediably distorted by the circumstances of his time. In doing this, we fail to observe that the norms he analysed—individualism, egalitarianism, law and order—are still fundamental to our own political life. If we overlook this fact, or regard it as only a minor aspect, we effectively prevent any genuine revival of theory.

What, then, are the prerequisites for such a revival? The greatest obstacle to a genuine revival is our failure to recognize what (and how much) we have in common with our ancestors. Preoccupied with vast material changes as well as great changes in political structures, we fail to notice how profound are the continuities. The essential subject-matter of political theory is to be found in enduring motivations or norms. It is their order of importance that has changed, not their collective significance for us. To revive theory, we must revise it not because the classical theorists were 'wrong', but because their concepts differ in non-basic ways from ours.

It might be argued that in view of such differences it would be better to ignore past theories and think anew. But this would show a failure to understand the importance of classical insights. The analyses contributed by classical theorists are at least as good as any that the modern mind can achieve. But we cannot just repeat what they said and suppose that the way we are thinking now is the way they would think if they were living today. Their views had a practical application to their own society, since those views arose from challenges to that society. If we are to revive their theory, we must use their ideas and concepts more as templates for recommendations having practical application today. The revival of theory is the restoration of its practical application.

The modernist plea for such a revival cannot of course mean an unqualified advocacy of the revival of classical concepts. Reconsideration of traditional concepts does not necessarily imply *their* revival—but the revival of theory as a mode of thought and a form of argument.

Chapter I

Is the Social Contract Obsolete?

A paradoxical fate for a theory is that it should be abandoned as a doctrine about the past or an explanation of the present, only to re-emerge as a practical proposal for the future. Such has been the case with the theory of the social contract. Attempts to re-examine it seriously have been few.[1] Yet virtually every major proposal for coping with international disorder is in effect a suggestion to apply a form of social contract: the argument runs that for their own good, theoretically equal and independent nations should bind themselves into a society, or place themselves under a super-government, capable of keeping peace and promoting the general welfare. Organizations such as the League of Nations and the United Nations have been set up, and have received the clear support of many who would consider a serious analysis of the classical theory a waste of time. It is curious that although democratic societies have neglected the social contract in dealing with their internal problems, they have at one and the same time been ready to advocate a contract as a solution to problems of external relations. There is an obvious contradiction here: if the social contract is an unsatisfactory historical fiction, it can hardly be

[1] In 1963 in France Edgar Faure launched an idea of a new social contract which in 1970 led to the formation of a society to study the problems of political reforms. See Edgar Faure, *Pour un nouveau contrat social* (Seuil, Paris, 1973). Another exception is the United Kingdom where early in 1974 the term 'social contract' was given new currency to describe an unwritten pact between trade unions and the government in the pre-election period. The unions were expected to observe certain constraints in their demands for wage increases. In exchange they had the Labour Party's commitment to extend the nationalisation of industry, to increase taxation of the rich, and to increase welfare benefits. Thus the new 'social contract' focused sharply on the trade unions and their newly-won central role in the power structure.

made into a satisfactory reality in the future; if it is of value in international relations, then not all that is comprised in its classical version can be obsolete.

Individual Values v Social Order

The neglect of the social contract theory appears particularly curious if one looks at one of the theory's unique features—its consistency with two sets of values: individualism and social order. The theory is successful where its best known alternatives—one claiming that government was established as a result of the power-hunger of a stronger force and the other that it came as an extension of the family—are not; for under the alternative theories government and society become either irrelevant (if an extension of the family) or at odds with the members of society (if imposed). This conflict between the members of society and the social order has not yet been solved by democracy. It remains both a theoretical difficulty and a practical problem.

The basis of this difficulty is that as a value individualism is hard to define and even more difficult to defend. Its affinities with egoism, together with its anarchistic implications, have made it repellent to many; and the ease with which it can be confused with the idea that man can exist independently of his society has made it appear absurd. Yet the notion persists that the individual human being has worth apart from any service he can perform or qualities he may possess. Similarly the assertion that government and society have moral worth has become a part of the democratic tradition. If one assumes that both values—individualism and social order—are held by the same person, government and society must then be seen as existing for the sake of the individual; but it is the nature of the relationship which is by no means clear and which presents a problem.

Among several positions that have been taken the most commonly held is the 'identity' theory, which removes the distinction between government and governed. According to this democratic solution the two can be made identical if certain ceremonial functions are performed. If some members of the public can stand for office and be voted into office by others, so the theory goes, the government becomes a government of the people; its function is to carry out the wishes of the public. Under these conditions government exists as a separate entity only as a convenience to members of the public who must give their main attention to other matters. One weakness of the 'identity' theory is that it makes the concept of government unintelligible: one cannot 'govern' oneself. There is also an implied threat to individualism, for whatever the intention of its advocates, it is an anti-individualist theory of the state. It justifies all government acts—which must often be anti-individualist because a government is concerned with reconciling private impulses with public directions—on the grounds that the acts are those of the people in general. Paradoxically, then, the erosion of individual rights may result from the assumption that a democratic government by definition cannot erode individual rights; it 'represents' the people.

Under another democratic solution, the 'agential' theory of government[2]—which is really a type of contract theory—members of the government are considered agents of the people, or 'public servants'. As with the master–servant relation, or agential relation, an implicit contract exists by which the servant or agent binds himself to carry out his master's wishes. In reality, however, there is no resemblance between an agent in law and the members of a government; for the man who employs an agent is legally responsible for his acts, whereas no such relation exists between voters and their government. It is not—alas!—the voters who are arraigned when incompetents or blackguards are elected to office. The image of an agent acting on behalf of a master who must eventually submit to the agent's orders does little to explain the relationship between government and the governed. Furthermore, this type of contract theory also is anti-individualistic, for the contract in this case is between one individual—the elected member—and the majority of voters, rather than between

[2] An attractive formulation was given by Paul Louis Courier in 1820: the 'coach-driver theory of democracy'. See Yves R Simon, *Philosophy of Democratic Government* (University of Chicago Press, Chicago, 1961), p 147.

individual members of the society and the government.

As the social contract theorists were fully aware, individualism is a non-social value and can easily become anti-social. The problem they faced was: how is it possible to reconcile the belief that individual members of society are the only real value-units with recognition of the worth of government and society? In other words: what relations between individuals and society can be postulated? Sometimes the question was posed in terms of obligation, sometimes in terms of freedom, but it can always be reduced to a conflict between two values: individualism and social order.

The problem can of course be ignored by disregarding one side of the argument. Administrators pursuing efficiency and convenience, utopian schemers searching for a simple solution, and those prone to follow conventional opinion have always been ready to dismiss individualism as an aberration or illusion; there are also many individualists who try to simplify their lives by refusing to admit the claims of society. Such 'solutions' ignore the fact that in our social system both types of values—individual and societal—are present. It is hardly possible not to apply at times one's own criteria of what is ultimately 'good', or to deny categorically that some kind of society and government is of benefit to the individual.

The conflict in values which the social contract theory was intended to solve has also been dismissed in effect by democratic society, which has reduced individualism to a set of 'rights' upheld by a constitution. So long as the prescribed 'rights'—the argument goes—are observed by the government, members of the society are obligated to obey its decrees no matter what the demands of self-interest may be; the society is good because it upholds individualism; hence no problem exists. Ironically, this contention has no persuasive effect on the problem-child himself—the individualist who denies that it is possible to prescribe a set of comprehensive rights for all time that will meet all the requirements of individualism. He will feel keenly the absurdity of being given by law the right to carry a revolver down Fifth Avenue while being denied the right to take himself and his toothbrush to China.

The democratic 'solution' to the conflict in values—and

much of the present neglect of the social contract is due to this supposed solution—is an illusion based on a misconception. Sir Ernest Barker argues that 'In days when government was still held to be *sui generis*, and to stand over against subjects as something of a separate order, it was natural to think that there was, or should be, a contract between them which fixed their mutual limits. Today the government is not *sui generis*; it is just a part of the legal association, as the body of general citizens is equally a part; and its rights and duties are fixed, like those of the citizens generally, under and by the one and only contract of the constitution.'[3]

Barker's statement does not recognize the seriousness of the conflict between the individualist value and government. No set of prescribed rights can meet all the requirements of individualism, for according to the latter it is the individual who decides his rights, not society. Nor can the 'rights' entirely restrict a government whose duty is to society as a whole: a government that concerns itself exclusively with individual 'rights' will cease to be a government. Furthermore, it is not true that the rights and duties of a government are 'fixed'. In a dynamic world they cannot remain fixed without the government's ceasing to perform its duties adequately. On the whole, then, it is not correct that democracy has solved—or even adequately investigated—the problem of the conflict between individualism and social order; but if the democratic argument were to envisage a new and revised form of social contract, some satisfactory answers might be found.

Individualism, the Social Contract and Constitutionalism

Discussing Sir Ernest Barker's attempt to retain the concept of contract ('political contract') by regarding the constitution as 'the articles of a contract which constitutes the State', J W Gough remarks that 'one cannot help feeling that the motive

---

[3] Sir Ernest Barker, Introduction to *Social Contract: Essays by Locke, Hume, and Rousseau* (Oxford University Press, New York, 1960), p xiv.

for doing so is at bottom a sentimental one—a reluctance to part company with an historic idea which has for so long been associated with cherished political ideals.'[4] Gough himself prefers to view constitutional government as a 'trusteeship', for such a term is 'free from many of the misleading associations of the contract theory.'[5] In other words, Gough feels that the contract theory is so beset with difficulties that it is best avoided even as a metaphor.

Some may feel that the question of what metaphor to apply is too trivial to merit consideration; to them, it is the essence of constitutional government which is of dominant importance. But a study of Gough's historical account of the contract theory's rise and fall shows a close association between a commitment to individualism and acceptance of the social contract. Gough explicitly mentions this association: 'In Spencer', he says, 'as in so many of his predecessors, individualism led inevitably to the contract theory of political obligation.'[6] The contract theory's traditional role 'had been as a defence of the rights of individuals against the government, but the effect of revolutionary tradition was to allow more and more power to the state. Nothing must stand in the way of the will of the sovereign people . . .'[7] Quoting Barker with approval, he says: 'If we hold that individual personality is the one intrinsic value of human life, we shall have no very great reason to fling stones at a theory which rested on a similar basis.'[8]

The reason for the close connection between individualism and the contract theory, and its implications for political theory, must now be investigated. There is also the question whether mere respect for constitutional government or the substitution of another 'metaphor' would be sufficient to preserve individualism. Those who feel that the metaphor issue is irrelevant should remember that in raising it we are really asking whether one should disregard the fact that the concept of constitutionalism developed from the contract theory.

[4] J W Gough, *The Social Contract* (Clarendon Press, Oxford, 1957), p 252.
[5] *Ibid*, p 255.
[6] *Ibid*, p 214.
[7] *Ibid*, p 205.
[8] *Ibid*, p 250.

In order to realize that the contract theory is inextricably linked with individualism one must consider the relationship between individual and government under the initial individualist assumption. Thus, given that the individual takes precedence over government and society (in both time and value), and given that the institution of government is good, its 'goodness' must stem from the individual's recognition of his government, which is another way of saying that he must choose the latter. To avoid the mistaken idea that one can govern oneself, the government is recognized as a separate entity and the relationship between the individual and his government is considered contractual: one consents to be governed even though one may not agree with every law passed by the government. In this relationship, the standards of right and wrong are still those of the individual, but the government is not simply a device for carrying out the desires of individual members. It is a separate body acting in the interest of all, a group whose decisions members of the body politic have contracted to accept. Just how this contract was established and what conditions it postulated are moot points; yet the problems posed cannot be dismissed, since no other theory can satisfy the requirements of both 'government' and 'individualism'.

It has been argued by Barker and Gough that constitutionalism is a modern substitute for the contract which disposes of the difficulties inherent in the traditional theory. But one cannot avoid the problems of contract theory unless one divorces the constitution and constitutionalism from their source in contract theory. The 'constitution' then becomes a statement about the legal rights and duties of government and governed as separate (although related) entities. Presumably no one is a party to such a constitution: it is simply a framework of rules within which society operates. It will change as society changes.

To be a genuine substitute for the contract theory this concept must be capable of explaining how individualism can continue to exist in a democratic society. In a way constitutionalism does attempt to explain this by arguing that a democratic society can dispense with the contract theory because all essential values are built into its institutions and legal codes. But the problem is that legal guarantees and institutional mores guarantee nothing in the long run: to assert that they do is to imply that society does not change.

For all this, seeing constitutionalism as a substitute for a contract has certain advantages. It has the merit of describing how a society really operates, for it removes the problem of adapting the legal conception of contract to a situation—that of having been born into a state—which does not provide the possibility of choice essential to the legal concept. The constitutional approach keeps close to the known fact that members of both the government and the public have grown up within a framework of assumptions: certain things can be done by each and certain things cannot. The public 'obeys' for the same reason that the government governs. Observation of the facts reveals what each is and does, so that no problem of interpretation exists.

One would have expected issues of this kind to have been a natural field of investigation for a behaviourally-oriented political scientist. However, as Giovanni Sartori has pointed out,[9] a behaviouralist, with his predilection for informal processes and his fear of formal structures, is not equipped to deal with the problem.[10] If we link the latter circumstance to the modern political science's avoidance of classical issues—such as the social contract—we realize the full extent of the present impasse in theorizing: behaviouralism makes the study of some modern concepts as superfluous and irrelevant as the analysis of concepts belonging to the classical tradition.

---

[9] Giovanni Sartori, 'Constitutionalism: A Preliminary Discussion', *The American Political Science Review*, vol LVI, no 4 (December 1962), p 863.

[10] Despite its wanderings into the history of political theory, Heinz Eulau's paper in Ithiel de Sola Pool (ed), *Contemporary Political Science: Toward Empirical Theory* (McGraw-Hill, New York, 1967) has not proved the contrary. *Nomos X: Representation* (1968), a publication of the American Society for Political and Legal Philosophy, implicitly exposes the poverty of behaviouralism in this respect.

Contractualism v Relativism and Individualism v Egalitarianism

What is the place of individualism in modern society? Individualism—or rather elements of it—has certainly been given some legal expression in the 'rights' and 'freedoms' granted to the members of democratic societies by their constitutions. But because there is an incompatibility between individualism and egalitarianism (the former being in some instances a denial of the latter's validity) and because egalitarianism occupies a special position in defining the forms of democratic institutions, individualism cannot be given explicit legal recognition to as great an extent. It must remain a mere qualification of what the society says about equality. Being a denial that all men can logically be treated as equal in every respect, individualism is not likely to survive in an egalitarian society if it is not supported by something more than the legal code. Unless there is a tacit agreement among the members of society that the individual—and not the majority—is the fundamental unit of value and source of value judgements, it is difficult to see how individualist values can be preserved. The importance of the social contract becomes clear: if one assumes the individual to be the ultimate unit and the institution of government to be good, one is committed to the contract theory. Conversely, acceptance of the contract theory is a commitment to individualism or, to put it differently, an implicit denial that the majority is always right and that relativism is an adequate philosophy.

Can individualism be preserved by a 'way of life', a 'tradition' or 'habitual behaviour'? None of these can ensure the continuation of any value in an egalitarian society other than egalitarianism, for an egalitarian society commits itself to relativism. A defence of individualism is provided by the social contract theory. Thus, when insisting that habitual behaviour should not be regarded as the sole determinant of obedience, the modern contractualist wishes to introduce a normative element into discussions of society. He opposes any attempt to exploit a factual description of the behavioural pattern, because this makes obedience easy to obtain through manipulation: a government faced by disaffection can learn from social scientists how to cope with it: how (through some form of 'brainwashing') to obtain 'consent' for any policy it wishes to pursue. Every contractualist must recognize that his view commits him to a non-relativist view of society. A contractualist can be defined as a non-relativist who wishes to introduce norms into the community without specifying the nature of those norms. The only way to do this is to assert that private conscience and the individual possessing it have ultimate value.

Unfortunately for the contractualist, it is not possible to convince his opposition that norms other than those present in his society would in some way be 'better'. One reason is that the concept of 'better' demands a standard of judgement common to both adverse critics of the system and those who are content with it. (It is to the latter category that the relativist in effect belongs.) Those who advocate a particular set of values, or a view of society which implies one, are no longer faced simply with the task of convincing others that their set of norms is 'better'; they must also convince those who deny that it is possible to debate the relative merits of different norms in any meaningful, scientific fashion, and who therefore insist that norms be excluded from the realm of discourse and analysis. Those who practise such exclusion, the relativists, have the support of both modern science and most philosophers in Britain and America. It is simply not possible to defend any particular set of values without taking some prior and basic normative statements as 'given'. The contractualist must be quite clear and honest about this. He must be quite frank that it is not possible to prove that there are values beyond what society allows to exist. Unfortunately it is not unusual for contractualists to be wary and clearly nervous about their position: thus when arguing for an ethical system within the concept of contract, John Rawls and J F A Taylor fail to suggest a clear content for the system. The reason is obvious. Even Rawls's simple 'justice as fairness' in its original version was demolished by Everett W Hall's attack.[11] Taylor, for all his desire to 'avoid sentimentality in this matter' could similarly be disposed of if any relativist cared to challenge it. One must not pretend otherwise. Contractualism must be recognised as a method of countering the relativism implicit in a purely egalitarian value order. What the contractualist must learn is to meet boldly the relativist charge of sentimental subjectivity by pointing out that relativism is also based on a value—equality. It is certainly not sounder philosophically than a view based on individualism, as contractualism is.

The non-relativist may feel that the relativist's position is rather curious, in that while the relativist says he does not care what the norms are, he takes a firm stand against any attempt to change them. For him, evidently, activities such as ordering, integrating and rationalising norms are disallowed. Like the linguist who feels that the grammarian's attempts to give a rational order to language are a violation of the nature of language, the relativist insists that the critic leave his society's norms alone. Such a position is of course normative, and is inevitably related to some fundamental norm adopted by the society to which the relativist belongs. The most obvious norm is the egalitarian view that the ultimate standard of value is the vox populi.

The value of a social contract theory is that it affirms that there are certain principles necessary to human associations and that it is impossible for a 'just' society to ignore or abandon them. How much 'content' for justice does Rawls provide in his *opus magnum*, which is a definitive statement of his modernized theory of the Social Contract?[12] The principles Rawls sets forth resemble the traditional principles of democratic societies. The validity of the particular set of norms suggested by him—which is fundamental to both human society and individuality—does not constitute his main contribution to political philosophy. The interesting point is that in an age of relativism he implies

---

[12] John Rawls, *A Theory of Justice* (Harvard University Press, Cambridge, 1971).

[11] See John Rawls, 'Justice as Fairness', *The Journal of Philosophy*, vol LIV, no 22 (October 1957), pp 653–62; Everett W Hall, 'Justice as Fairness: a Modernized Version of the Social Contract', *ibid*, pp 662–70; and John F A Taylor, *The Masks of Society* (Appleton-Century-Crofts, New York, 1966). See also section below on Rawls.

that there are clear limits to relativism[13]—that if one is to believe in relativism one can do so only within a framework which is normative.

Rawls's theory of the social contract offers a theoretical justification for constitutionalism: at no point can a just society insist that democratic principles—the majority will, abstract equality, abstract liberty, 'necessity'—require it to abandon its constitution. Thus the contract theory gives justice its 'standard' meaning—which is not the same as supplying a 'content'.

The very nature of the 'social contract' and 'standard justice' require that options for their content be left open. This would pose no problem if society were normatively oriented, or if one believed that since there are some inviolable principles, there must be others. But if a society has adopted relativism—as is the case with the democratic societies—the following problems may arise. Firstly, the fundamental assumptions of contract theory may be questioned on the ground that being non-relativistic they must be false. Secondly, if accepted on the basis of their 'fundamentality', they may be offered as the only alternative—the only assumption that one should make. As a result, society regards a mere outline of justice as justice itself; it accepts a 'contentless' kind of justice—a framework which can be filled at will. This is why society today is torn by extraordinary conflicts: thus the abstract principle of 'freedom' makes people insist on their 'rights' and the satisfaction of their demands, regardless of what it would cost the community. Consequently, if one were to recognize that democratic principles form merely an outline, a framework, and do not represent the total normative content, such problems would not arise. Nor could anyone argue—as so many do nowadays—that as long as an act is not illegal, it is justifiable. It is not for law to promulgate norms but rather to create the conviction that normative (principled, rational) behaviour is the only behaviour acceptable to a human community. 'Rational choice' together with consideration of oneself and one's relations with others, that form the

---

[13] Without specifically discussing relativism, Rawls recognizes its problems when he talks of 'intuitionism': 'intuitionism is not constructive' etc (*Op cit*, p 52). To him, 'intuitionism' implies a plurality of 'first principles' of right action (pp 34 ff).

basis of a hypothetical contract, must continue to operate in a society. It is the necessary conditions for such a choice that Rawls's social contract theory prescribes and this is as far as its 'general content' takes us.

Obligation and Consent in the Social Contract

In Part One of his article 'The Logic of Social Contracts' J F M Hunter questions whether it is desirable to think of relations between government and governed in terms of a social contract. He concludes that for many reasons such a theory is best avoided.[14]

Hunter begins his argument against the contract theory by asserting that the date when the hypothetical contract is made is irrelevant—unless within the living generation—since 'one person cannot contractually bind another'. He acknowledges two exceptions—the power of attorney and long-term property leases which bind the heirs—but disregards the fact that the exceptions to the rule are universal. No private contract binds the contracting parties alone. Apart from such obvious examples as the binding of children by the parents' marriage contract and the binding of a dissident, even revolutionary government by the contracts of the very government it replaces—both of which are analogous to the terms of traditional contract theory in their emphasis on legitimacy—it seems clear that the terms of private contracts require recognition by both jurists and the public. Unless contracts specify that their terms are subject to a time limit, they remain valid and cover successors to those who were parties to the original agreement. Without this requirement, all contracts would have to be reviewed whenever a birth or death occurred. Even if we believe the original agreement to have been made wrongfully—as with the allegedly extravagant land grants made to

---

[14] 'It would be extremely cumbersome to keep the contract alive; neither citizen nor government would gain from it anything of value which they did not already possess or which could be achieved only in this way. And it would appear to ossify the social structure unduly.' J F M Hunter, 'The Logic of Social Contracts', *Dialogue*, vol V (1966), no 1, pp 36–7.

the Canadian Pacific Railway before 1900, or where the contract was made by illegitimate predecessors—the case is not altered.

With reference to the important problem of consent, Hunter argues that consent to a contract does not make citizens do willingly what they must do in any event, because 'tacit consent never argues willingness' and 'explicit consent need not be so'. He refers to a dilemma of tacit consent and speaks of his inability 'to prove that there is no conceivable solution to difficulties'.[15] Nonetheless, he remains hostile because 'even if one did succeed in hammering out a solution, it would be evident that the solution was guided by, devised to satisfy, a prior conviction . . .', and 'if we independently have answers . . . we do not need a social contract theory.'[16]

It appears that Hunter wishes to convey the following: since it is possible to explain obligation without a social contract theory and because the theory involves troublesome problems of interpretation, it should be rejected. If this is what Hunter means, his argument misses the point. It is true that social contract theories are theories of political obligation, but they are not formulated merely to explain obligations. Indeed, the obligations contained in them are not expressed solely in terms of the legal requirements of contracts. Obligation is a problem not because it is difficult to understand why men obey their governments, but because it is impossible to justify obligation without a theory of contract if both individualism and government are accepted as values.

The problem can be evaded either by abandoning one of these values, or by denying that the word 'value' as it has been used here has any meaning. This is usually the modern philosophic solution, and accounts to some degree for the neglect of contract theories today. The relativist may argue that since values are but tastes and attitudes selected from those available within a culture, there can be no conflict. The non-relativist is not in this happy position. Although he may have great difficulty in proving that the values he works with are absolutes, or even necessary to his culture, he nonetheless believes that

[15] *Ibid*, p 35.
[16] *Ibid*, pp 35–6.

values have preceded the particular culture in which they are found and have profoundly affected its form; to him they are not simply descriptions of what men do, but goals for which they strive and which they attempt to mould into rational patterns. It is therefore impossible for him to accept that analyses of habit patterns, or the simple incorporation of 'rights' in a legal document, do anything to solve the major problem posed by contract theory.

Contractual and Representative Views of Government and the 'Prisoner's Dilemma'

Although Runciman and Sen maintain[17] that the 'prisoner's dilemma' was first devised by A W Tucker and discussed by Luce and Raiffa in *Games and Decisions* (1957), conceptions of it have certainly existed in man's consciousness for a much longer time. Abstractly expressed, the dilemma implies that in a social situation—consisting of like members whose private decisions affect each other's position—even a wholly rational being cannot act in his own best interest unless someone outside that situation compels him to do so. In essence, this is the argument that Hobbes used to support the propositions that covenants without the sword are but words, and that the sovereign cannot be a party to the social contract. It is the light which the dilemma throws on contract theory that is its principal contribution.

The need for a contract theory arises when a law passed by the government conflicts with the individual's wishes. When the individual protests against the law, he is in effect objecting that the government is not acting in the way he wants it to behave and as individualism declares it ought to. If his objections cannot be met, he tends to become a rebel who violates those laws which he finds distasteful; moreover, the political system begins to break down, for no matter how strong the

[17] See W G Runciman and Amartya K Sen, 'Games, Justice and the General Will', *Mind*, vol LXXIV (October 1965), pp 554–62.

forces of habit and convention are, man will not indefinitely fulfill requirements which do not make sense to him. Something like this is happening with large numbers of people today: they obey only what they are compelled to obey.

Frequent attempts are made to answer the objections of individuals by appealing to democratic principles of fairness. It is argued that the citizen has agreed to a bargain: given the chance of having his wishes carried out, by voting for a party that has a platform agreeable to him, he must accept the consequence that his desires will sometimes not be fulfilled, since he is living in a community with conflicting interests, each member of which has made the same bargain. This view has all the weaknesses of the original contract theory: when did the citizen make such a bargain? and so forth. And it has the additional weakness of being uncertain. The citizen has apparently made a contract that he must honour, but which will not necessarily satisfy any conditions: in other words, there is no guarantee that his interests will ever be considered.

The 'prisoner's dilemma' provides an answer by showing that because of my position and my inability to expect assistance from others, unless we are all compelled to cooperate, I am not as capable of independently pursuing my own interest as I suppose. I need a government that does not simply carry out my wishes as I see them. The importance of Runciman and Sen's discussion of games theory and the General Will lies in its demonstration that in some social situations the sum of private interests is not the same as the public interest—which supplies an argument for a contractual rather than a representative view of government.

Representative government has often been described as contractual, but a distinction should be noted. The early model of representative government is the direct democracy of classical Greece, which is adapted to large states via the fiction that the decision-making body in some way 'represents' or 'is like' the public and consequently will decide issues as the public would presumably decide them if it maintained its identity as a democratic government. Contractual or responsible government, on the other hand, need not employ the direct democracy model. Serving its needs is the concept of a legal contract based on the fiction that sometime, somehow, the members of the body politic became parties to a contract. In terms of plausibility there is little to choose between the two fictions. What matters is their ability to solve the problems posed by the democratic premises and entailed by the democratic acceptance of individualism: specifically, questions about freedom and obedience in the relations between government and the individual.

An advocate of the representative view of government attempts to explain obedience as a non-philosophical Greek might have done: I obey a law that is not in my interest because I accept the system under which such laws are established. I accept the system because it is the only one consistent with the principle of equality which permits me as a general rule to have my own views enacted into law, even though at any one time I may be in the minority and thus fail to have my views embodied in legislation. The difficulty is that this argument makes sense only in the case of a small homogeneous community where differences in viewpoint would indeed reflect individuality rather than permanent differences in interests and values. Applied to the system of representative government in a large state it becomes misleading. A 'representative' cannot fully 'represent' individuals. At best he can 'represent' but a small part of me and occasionally act in my interest when new legislation is proposed; but this happens so seldom that it is not rational for me to obey laws based on such a system.

The theory of contractual government, as manifested in the 'prisoner's dilemma', says in effect that I 'obey' the government because what it commands is what I would have done if I were capable of ensuring that others would act as I am required to act: that is, government is a device for obtaining the cooperation we recognize as advantageous. Unfortunately, the argument holds only so long as there is no conflict of interest between me and the rest of the community: the 'dilemma' is a non-zero-sum game. So long as cooperation involves no loss for the individual members of the body politic—obviously a rare situation—the concept of public interest is perfectly clear: it is what each member would want if he could be assured of the cooperation of others in getting it. The government can make decisions because it knows what the public interest is; the public 'obeys' because it knows that the government understands the nature of the public interest, and because it has a clear-cut way of telling whether the government is acting in accordance with that interest. But when there are clashes of interest between the members of a society, contractual government can no longer find any definition of public interest; consequently, it has no way of making logical decisions and discharging its professed function. Where there are conflicting interests, representative government is in no better position than contractual government. Since by definition it would have to 'represent' the conflicts, it could solve them only by introducing a non-representative principle.

Uses of the 'Prisoner's Dilemma'

The limits of the situations comprehended by the 'prisoner's dilemma' are obvious. It does not describe decision-making situations which include ethical considerations (eg to steal or not to steal); nor does it apply to situations where there is a conflict of interest, since the non-cooperative situation which it describes specifically implies the possibility of cooperation, which a clash of interest rules out. Nonetheless, the 'prisoner's dilemma' provides a very valuable analytical tool and a convenient way of discussing contract theories: not only because it uses widely accepted modern terms, but also because it makes us keenly aware of our premises and their limitations. The dilemma refers only to those situations in which we would like to cooperate because we can foresee the advantages of concerted action, but where the latter is unobtainable without some kind of coercion from without. Possibly—especially in a modern megalopolitan society—this is a common situation. It should be remembered, however, that the dilemma says nothing about the exact nature of the government beyond the fact that in the situations referred to it cannot be representative. Although it suggests that the government is capable of acting in the public interest, it provides no definition of 'public interest' and can therefore give no assurance that the government will in fact act in accord with that interest.

Chapter II

The General Will and the Public Interest

It would be easy to say that the neglect of Rousseau's concept of the General Will is his fault rather than ours, that his fondness for rhetoric and distaste for philosophical niceties has made more sober thinkers reject it as an illusion. But concepts in the social sciences are not merely descriptions of things—or of relationships—that are present to the eye of a careful observer. Even if originally they are not valid, they can—if believed in—so affect behaviour that they do in fact become accurate descriptions of it. If the General Will has been discarded, we must look for an explanation other than the supposedly unreal nature of the description it gives.

Transformation of the General Will

No doubt Rousseau's insistence that the General Will operates only under conditions that do not prevail in the present overgrown states has done little to make his work seem relevant today, and the peculiar difficulty in English of making his distinction between the General Will and the will of all has not helped matters. Not only does 'general will' in English seem to be an abbreviation of 'will of the general (public)' but the egalitarian value-order leads us to assume that the will of the general public ought to serve the same function as Rousseau's General Will; that is, if we use the term at all we are likely to use it to refer to what Rousseau called the will of all.

In a democracy, it is easy to assume that the ultimate standard of the good is what everyone wants or agrees upon and that the goal for which one should strive is a consensus. The common good becomes the consensus on what is the common good, for if it is right that all should decide issues, a decision reached in any other way would be wrong. (Otherwise it would be wrong for all to decide issues.) Rousseau, however, in distinguishing between the General Will and the will of all, and in linking justice with the General Will rather than the will of all, would seem to have specifically excluded any interpretation of the General Will in the sense of a consensus. The result of the peculiarities of the English language, then, and of our tendency to identify the good with popular opinion and popular choice is that for the relativists the General Will becomes an obscure term for what can be more clearly expressed by 'consensus'; while for the non-relativists the distinction becomes hopelessly confusing.

More important in understanding the neglect—perhaps even the repudiation—of Rousseau's terminology is our association of the concept of General Will with totalitarian rather than democratic states. If one thinks of the General Will as requiring somebody to do the willing (ie a will implies a willer), the ground is laid for postulating the state as separate from individuals: the organic conception of the state. It is not simply because democracies have been in conflict with states holding the organic view that the organic conception has never been entirely acceptable to them. From the days of the Reformation, which set out the rights of private conscience in opposition to the claims of the Church and rejected the argument that the clergy could be corrupt while the Church remained incorruptible, the notion that an institution or legal entity could have an existence apart from its members has been anathema to upholders of the protestant-democratic tradition. The emphasis on personal salvation and personal sin within this tradition has made it difficult to accept the idea that institutions of any kind may have an existence separate from that of their members. The individualism inherent in the concept of private salvation has also hindered belief in a body superior to its components; finally, it was the scientific reluctance to multiply entities needlessly that has nourished an atomistic conception of society: the whole—it was contended—is simply never greater than its parts. In short, as our traditions are opposed to organic conceptions of the state, the General Will, in so far as it seems to entail one, is not acceptable.

The General Will does not, however, necessarily demand an organic conception of the state. If 'will' is detached from the organism and attached to a value order, if we conceive of will as the pursuit of goals rather than an attribute of personality, then there is no need to suppose that the General Will is organismic in its conception or totalitarian in its implications. Yet such an interpretation of the General Will will not come readily, since it makes sense only under a non-relativistic conception of values.

The General Will and Totalitarianism

There is an interesting identification of the General Will by E F Carritt who argues that the question of 'ought' can be answered only 'in terms of [man's] obligations to his fellow man'; he then contrasts this sense with 'an inspiration of the National Spirit [called] the General Will', which, he says, 'is what an earlier age . . . called the Will of God . . . or a later, unashamed of naked materialism, the Dictatorship of the Proletariat.'[1]

This kind of identification needs to be carefully examined, for it has long served as an argument for adherents of utilitarianism and relativism, and advocates of greater popular control over government decisions. What Carritt at first seems to be saying is that whenever the answer to 'ought' goes beyond the immediate desires of the members of a body politic, the absolute standard implied can be called what you want—Reason, the Will of God or the General Will—but it remains what you do not want, the justification for totalitarian imposition of an arbitrary standard. In other words, the identification seems to imply that a genuinely democratic régime is by its nature committed to some form of utilitarianism or relativism.

The position is very plausible. Obviously, if a distinction can be made between the General Will and the private will so that the collective private will—the will of all—is not necessarily the

[1] E F Carritt, *Ethical and Political Thinking* (Clarendon Press, Oxford, 1947), p 144.

same as the General Will, the door seems open to some form of totalitarianism: enforcement of the good by decree, or by the manipulation of mind and conscience under the guise of education.

At this point one must be especially careful—which many critics of Rousseau are not. It is not the claim that there is an absolute standard superior to relativist or utilitarian standards that makes Rousseau the 'father' of modern totalitarianism; it is his failure to supply a clear and plausible explanation of how that standard is to be determined. Absolutes do not imply their imposition.

Indeed, we already have in scientific statements about reality a set of beliefs and values that are as close to being absolute truths as any authoritarian could wish for. Yet one could not reasonably claim that the system is arbitrarily imposed on a reluctant set of believers, or that it could be so imposed and still remain what it professes to be. In the moral sphere or the sphere of decisions about human behaviour and directions, the act of faith that an equally absolute set of standards could exist is not in itself a totalitarian assumption. What matters is how the standard is to be known. If the General Will is, as Carritt suggests, a matter of 'inspiration', and if it implies that the source of obligation is not 'to be sought by reason', we must conclude that the General Will is totalitarian. It is not the existence of an absolute standard over and above the interests of the masses or even the postulation of a Wise Legislator that establishes totalitarian conditions, but the absence of a method by which private conscience can validly question the standard or decisions of the legislator. So long as moral issues and social questions can be decided only on the basis of intuition or inspiration, there is no possibility of a régime being other than totalitarian, whatever its institutional form. Democracy becomes at best simply the tyranny of the majority. But if the absolute is reached by means other than intuition, revelation and so forth, and it can be shown that the concept of the General Will is not necessarily intuitive by nature, it is difficult to regard it either as the forerunner of later totalitarian concepts or the campfollower of earlier ones.

The attempt to find parallels between Rousseau's General

Will and marxist-communist theory must result in a misleading analysis of the basic differences between democracy and communism. The analysis encourages naïve liberals and prevents the development of an adequate theory of modern democratic government: the drawing of parallels reduces the issue between the two systems to a difference between a system of government in which the wishes of the people decide policy and one in which an oligarchy does. It is the distaste of the liberal critic for any theory which denies that the ultimate and sole standard of government is the wishes of the governed that makes him ready to attack Rousseau and argue that governments whose policies are obviously repugnant to our society have their antecedents and justification in his theories. But the issues dividing communism and democracy cannot be reduced to libertarianism, to the simplified view that in one society the members are free to act on impulse whereas in the other they are compelled to act against it. The real problem confronting us is to evolve a sound theory of responsible government that is not also a defence of totalitarianism. A concept of the General Will which incorporates respect for the individual and allows scope for a theory of natural law entailing something more than a mere will of all, seems to offer one possibility.

The difficulty is that Rousseau, as A Cobban says, 'comes close to identifying natural law with the general will. In so far as this identification is assumed it means that the idea of Natural Law ceases to be capable of playing its former role in the state as a moderating influence over political power.'[2] If so, Rousseau's view is very similar to the instrumental ethics of communism and must be held responsible for the repeated assertions of this similarity. The problem, however, is that in noting similarities within a society that specifically repudiates particular influences, we are not talking about real or direct relations. It is true that a man or society can specifically deny the worth or validity of an idea and still hold tenaciously to it. Thus, the atheist may be regarded as a believer. But when ideas are declared to be the product of circumstances rather

---

[2] Alfred Cobban, *Rousseau and the Modern State* (Allen & Unwin, London, 1964), p 169.

than sources—as they are in the communist ideology, despite the latter's rigidity—the links we see must be direct. There can be no doubt about Hegel's influence on Marx or the influence of the Christian value order on current Russian society. But such relationships are direct. To trace the source of the influence further is futile, except for the purpose of historical investigation; the study of sources is valuable only when ideas are recognized as genuine sources—as influences on human thought and behaviour. So long as one believes that ideas are genuine influences, Plato is worth investigating under conditions in which the source is still at work as a source. When, however, ideas are felt to be a by-product of action, they become orphans, understandable only in themselves. In our society, which has not committed itself wholly to pragmatism, Rousseau is capable of offering insights into the problem of, say, integrating the concept of responsible government with the original assumptions of democracy: that is, we can not only find elements of Rousseau's theories in modern ideas, but we have reason to believe that he can surprise us by adding to the 'family' of ideas. In communist societies, on the other hand, only study of the immediate family, parent and child, can give us insights into the state of society and its goals, for they have broken with the logic of history and the need for consistency in their efforts to decide which way they will go.

The General Will and Democracy

Apart from being too ambiguous to be generally employed in discussions of democratic theory, the General Will concept has caused democratic societies some embarrassment. Democracies have inherited a parliamentary system which has no room for a conception of justice separable from the public, the legislature, and the judiciary; and if the General Will cannot be identified with the will of any of these, it cannot—under a system which recognizes the sovereignty of one of these organs—serve the function ascribed by Rousseau. In the abstract the General Will is a perfectly sound proposition, but when incorporated into a working democratic system it undermines the institutional forms necessary to adapt democratic theory to actual conditions. If we begin with the assumptions that men are equal by nature, that private conscience is infallible when distinguishing between right and wrong, and that men are social rather than solitary creatures—propositions acceptable to both Rousseau and democratic theorists in general—it follows that a general will having precedence over private wills can and must exist. The hypothetical equality presumably abolishes the distinction between public and private. But men are not in fact equal, as Rousseau himself saw. He was quite ready to agree to Aristotle's declaration that some men are born to be slaves. Rousseau, however, said that Aristotle mistook the effect for the cause. 'If some men are by nature slaves,' he says, 'the reason is that they have been made slaves *against* nature.'[3]

Now where inequality exists, the concept of the General Will loses its logical connection with private conscience and public interest. It still can be considered a proposition about true justice, but its mode of operation becomes a matter of speculation rather than logic. When some men are less rational, less informed and less moral than others, when the claims of private interest override man's sense of public interest—as must be the case when operation of the egalitarian value sets men in competition—then the will of all cannot possibly be the General Will, as it theoretically could and would be if they had been equal. Rousseau of course made certain suggestions as to how the General Will was to be ascertained, and the conditions under which it would operate, but his reasoning is by no means convincing and there is the serious difficulty that the conditions he prescribed for its exercise never seem to exist. Furthermore, the conditions laid down by Rousseau undermine the institutional forms favourable to egalitarian theory. Acceptance of the General Will concept throws grave doubt on the validity of the majority rule principle and, according to Rousseau, the concept excludes representation. It is, then, not very surprising that the concept 'General Will' has not had much impact on actual working democracies.

[3] J-J Rousseau, *The Social Contract* (Sir Ernest Barker ed), (Oxford University Press, New York, 1960), p 172.

An important part in reviving interest in the legitimating possibilities of concepts related to Rousseau's General Will has been the need to harmonize traditional democratic theory with the concept of responsible government under the stimulus of defending the system against the theory of communism. The concept of 'responsible government' becomes inevitable if one recognizes that people are in fact not equal and therefore by no means the sole or best judges of their own interests. (Reinforcing this is the fact that even if equality did exist, a government elected by the majority would be an unjust government if it 'represented' that majority without consideration for the minority.) Although the term originated in the idea that a representative government must be responsible to the people in the sense of 'answerable to', the need for electing a government by majority vote, and for its being representative of the whole people, gave the word the sense it has in other contexts: morally reliable, able to distinguish right from wrong and act accordingly. This is the kind of responsibility people have in mind when they recognize as legitimate the appeal for a large majority made by a party seeking office, in order that it may be free from the compromises induced by factions and sectional interests. Responsible government, in short, is regarded as distinct from representative government. As such, it disposes of many of the common objections to democratic government: the tyranny of the majority; the impossibility of genuine representation; the relativism implicit in basing a government on the wishes of the people; the anarchy that may result from making one man's opinion as good as another's. In other words, it serves a function similar to that attributed by A D Lindsay to Rousseau's theory.[4] It achieves this, however, by means of the implicit assumption that a responsible government knows what the public interest is by virtue of having been elected to office. Somewhere in this concept of responsible government lies the solution to the ideological dilemma: how can we retain the traditional forms and procedures of democracy but rid them of anarchistic and relativistic implications? Since the concept is

---

[4] See A D Lindsay, *The Modern Democratic State* (Oxford University Press, New York, 1962), p 235.

definable in terms of public interest, some of the interpretations and implications of the latter should be examined.

Public Interest

In the past, the concept of a public interest not identical with the sum of private interests has received short shrift from theorists of democracy. Perhaps use of it might look too much like an attempt to rally support for a policy that the general public does not accept, or to defend what is in the interest of the government but not of anyone else. The utilitarian idea that the sum of private interests is the common interest has accorded much more with democratic individualism than the Rousseauian idea that the public interest is what remains after private interests have been eliminated. However, the concept of responsible government, which is not only a 'popular' but a 'governmental' conception, requires a re-examination of the utilitarian interpretation, for when action is required in the public interest, defining the latter as the sum of other interests entails the same kind of hopeless calculus that made utilitarianism impracticable. Interests are not simply additive; they often divide, and where there is such a division any attempt to use the conflict as a guide to action must be self-defeating.

So long as government was viewed as a merely regulatory body for maintaining peace and order, all that was expected from a truly democratic government was an inability to act other than through set procedures, in line with an established code and in a strictly limited area. The least government was the best. But the demands for an active rather than passive government, coupled with the necessary qualification that the action must not be simply in the government's own interest or that of interest groups alone, have created the need for a more adequate definition of public interest; and the need is becoming more and more obvious as the demands upon government grow.

Apart from the Benthamite interpretation of public interest as the sum of private interests—which, as Edgar Bodenheimer observes,[5] has to face the problem of ascertaining what the private interests are and deciding whether numerical weight should be the sole factor in making a decision—the concept has been given various interpretations. 'Public interest' has been identified with several notions: the policy decisions of the government—a view that makes all acts of government appear in the public interest and precludes criticism; the interests of the collective organism which, as Bodenheimer observes, must—because it can act only through human beings—meet the same objections as are levelled at the view that the state's acts are justified per se; and 'the cumulative content of statutory enactments'[6]—the 'constitution', as it were.

Much could be said against these interpretations, and much has been, but the immediate point is that all of them represent the classic assignment of sovereignty in democracies: the people, the legislature, the state, the 'constitution'. Clearly, when public interest is discussed, sovereignty is also being discussed; for in questioning whether acts are in accordance with the public interest, one is inevitably raising the question of who should govern. The public interest, like Rousseau's General Will, is right by definition and the problem is to ascertain precisely how to define it. Of equal significance is the fact that identifying the public interest with the total private interest of the public is now dismissed with little comment: it is an 'archaic' view, 'Benthamite' in its conception. The latter, too, is to be expected, for if this were all that the public interest meant, the possibility of regarding it as separate from majority rule would scarcely exist. It becomes significant only when doubts arise whether majority rule can always be right. Opposing popular opinion or majority decision to the public interest is like contrasting the will of all with the General Will. Similarly to the General Will, the device solves the same problems of rescuing democracy from the anarchy of individualist will and raises the same difficulties: how it is to be discovered and kept compatible with democracy rather than tyranny.

[5] See Edgar Bodenheimer, 'Prolegomena to a Theory of the Public Interest,' *NOMOS V: The Public Interest* (Atherton Press, New York, 1962), p 208.

[6] Bodenheimer, *art cit*, p 209.

Ironically, it seems that nothing emerges from analyses of public interest that attaches it firmly and exclusively to the traditions of democracy. The difficulty is that without the concept of public interest democracy is not tenable. Only if it can be shown that systems we call democratic states are the only kind that can act in the public interest, is it possible to defend them effectively.

To what extent has political theory been moving in this direction? The problem with the concept of the General Will as presented by theorists like Barker and Lindsay is that while they use the concept to make justice something more than the sum of public wants, they wish the public to remain fully aware of what the General Will is; to achieve this they have to attribute to the public qualities it does not possess. Barker's argument is that 'as the result of a *long-time* process of thought, moving in the area of Society and being therefore a process of *social* thought, there emerges a *common conviction which is also a general will* about a right order of human relations and the obligatory nature of that order.'[7] Elsewhere he states[8] that intellectual effort and moral abstinence are necessary to translate the wishes of the General Will into legislative measures. This kind of argument agrees with the notions of moral improvement under democracy that have sustained the hopes of optimists, but it is hardly realistic. To the charge that the public is too self-seeking and too uninformed about critical issues to be capable of promoting justice, it is no answer to say that in time, through sustained reflection and moral abstinence, it will be. It is precisely because it does not possess the needed qualities that objections to democracy are raised. If all men had the qualities they were once supposed to have—rationality in the eighteenth-century sense, and good will—there would be no need for a theory of the General Will. The majority would always reach just decisions. This is to say that Barker's theory serves no real purpose. It is no more than an admission that justice today is not the product of majority rule, coupled with the hope that

[7] Ernest Barker, *Principles of Social & Political Theory* (Clarendon Press, Oxford, 1951), pp 198–9.

[8] Ernest Barker, Introduction to *Social Contract: Essays by Locke, Hume, and Rousseau*, p xxxvii.

one day it will be.

Yet the real weakness in theories requiring an improvement in man's nature is not that they are unrealistic; it is that they strike at the very root of the democratic value-order by attacking individualism. Self-seeking individualism is the value that distinguishes democracy from totalitarianism and prevents democratic states from supposing that the good of the state—or of the public—should ever be exalted over that of its individual members. Individualism maintains that man is self-centred and that this is a good thing. He may not be as blindly egoistic as Hobbes supposed, but he can never be as altruistic or community-minded as Barker would like him to be without forcing us to give up our belief in individualism. In a democracy, the first interest of a man is himself, not the community. Unless a theory of the General Will recognizes this fact, it cannot be called a democratic theory.

But if it is a premise of democracy that self-interest is a good, what are we to make of a political order that requires the members of its government to act in the public interest rather than their own? Is this an illusion? Is democracy impossible because it requires that its members be subject to contradictory impulses? The answer is negative, unless we insist that the people must be sovereign and that what constitutes the public interest be determined by them alone. Under such conditions justice is simply not possible. If we are willing, however, to allow a democratically elected government to determine the public interest, and if we are ready to accept the concept of responsible government, it does seem possible; for although it is not usual for the private citizen to suppress his own interest for the sake of the common good, it is quite possible for the members of a government to make the desire to fulfill the public interest a part of their own self-interest. In a way this is already happening, although the tendency is impeded by the failure of theory to provide an adequate guide.

Although members of the general public have in fact very little say in who is to 'represent' them, the number of politicians and civil servants who make genuine sacrifices for the sake of holding office is probably quite large. Such men are by no means self-sacrificing, for there are certain rewards that their personalities require—a sense of service, public recognition, status, the satisfaction of wielding power; it is thus in their self-interest to make what other people would call 'sacrifices'. Despite the considerable scope for promoting personal economic interests, whether through graft or a knowledge of business opportunities, relatively few take advantage of it. The reason for the frequent exceptions to this—pork-barrel politics ('You favour me here and I'll favour you there') in North America, etc—should not concern us. The point is that a large number of men act in a way that would be altruistic among the rest of the community, but not because they are altruistic by nature. Rather, they regard the consequences of their behaviour as being in their own self-interest. Democratic government rests on this precarious foundation—a partial compromise between the private and public interests. Consequently, it is not sufficient that government members suppose they are acting in the public interest, or that the public believes they wish to do so. The public is rarely in a position to decide what is right and wrong, so that government acts should not be immediately subject to the public will. What is needed is that government acts should be carefully scrutinized for evidence of self-interest, stupidity, complacency and indifference; and that the evidence be remembered at the next election. This in turn requires that the public be cynical rather than wise, unforgiving rather than broad-minded, suspicious rather than trusting. When matters of public interest are at stake, this is surely not expecting too much.

Public Interest and a 'Mythologized' Rousseau

If one is talking of interest groups—which has been fashionable for some time—a conception of public interest is necessary, not simply because the conception of democracy requires it, but also because that of government does. If—from the government viewpoint—each man had rights and interests only to the extent to which he strove to assert them, it is quite certain that every man would do so. The system would demand the attitude

Hobbes postulated for the state of nature. We might suppose then that public apathy is characteristic of a democracy because most people are convinced that they need not form pressure groups or otherwise strive to influence the government in their favour. The government—they feel—is looking after their interests: that is, most citizens evidently feel that there is a public interest which is recognized by the government when it passes judgment on legislation advanced by special interest groups. Obviously, some method of deciding between conflicting interest groups is logically necessary and the deciding factor cannot be the 'power' of the group unless that group is to become in effect the sovereign power. A concept of public interest is clearly essential.[9] There must be a concept of public interest compatible with democratic relativism and related to democratic decision-making. It is apparent that the concept proposed by Brian Barry has a good deal of merit.

Barry offers a description of interest ostensibly designed to incorporate uses of interest ignored by group theorists: 'a policy, law or institution is in someone's interest if it increases his opportunities to get what he wants—whatever that may be.' The main point about the definition according to its author is that it 'is always a *policy* that is said to be "in so-and-so's interest"—not the actual manner in which he is impinged upon.'[10] I would contend that the 'main point' is that Barry's definition makes the goals of policy determinable by the people or interest groups while leaving the means to be determined by the government. In other words, ends and means, intrinsic and extrinsic values, are completely separated for him in the making of decisions by the state.

There is unquestionably something attractive in this view. In the first place, it is consistent with relativism and the democratic idea that the people must govern if the government is to

[9] Hence we can agree with Brian Barry that there is something seriously wrong with definitions of interest made by group theorists which either exclude the concept of public interest or make it a rare phenomenon. It is not, however, that these definitions ignore important considerations—as Barry implies—but that they make interest group interpretations of government unworkable.

[10] Brian Barry, 'The Public Interest', Anthony Quinton (ed), *Political Philosophy* (Oxford University Press, London, 1967), p 115.

be called democratic. It also solves the difficulty posed by those prone to define a democratic government as one elected by a universal franchise but not bound to execute the 'will' of the electorate. Such a view leaves the government without a policy-making method because it leaves it without norms, whereas Barry's approach retains the traditional source of norms while escaping the objection that the public is simply not able to govern itself, logically or in practice. Under his definition, it is perfectly possible for people to 'mistake their interests' and thus require a policy to be imposed for their supposed benefit—forced to be free in the Rousseau sense—because it is obvious that no man is a pansophist. He might know what he wants and a democratic government by nature will try to obtain it for him, but he certainly will not always know how to get it. A government is necessary, especially under modern conditions, to decide upon the 'how'.

It should be noted that Barry is remarkably 'friendly' toward Rousseau. He devotes a good deal of his paper to 'demythologizing' him, by which he means that if Rousseau's conception of the General Will can be shown to be consistent with his own idea of the public interest the objections to Rousseau can be exposed as a mythology. The success of Barry's efforts to identify the two can be judged by examining his analysis.

The difficulty with this conception of the public interest—and hence the difficulty with his 'demythologizing' effort—is that ends and means are necessarily separated when we are analysing the 'good', but are inseparable when we are analysing actual policy. Barry's account of public interest and democratic policy-making would be acceptable only if everyone agreed that the end justifies the means. (This is as necessary a precondition as that 'the only proposals to be taken into account when estimating "common interests" should be proposals which treat everyone affected in exactly the same way.'[11]) The reason it is a necessary condition is that if means are as important as—or more important than—ends, decisions about them must be made by those who decide the ends. Being deprived of the possibility of deciding the means, the people may protest

[11] *Ibid*, p 118.

that their interests are being only half served. It will be no answer to say that they cannot know the means. If one denies that someone else's concept of the good is relevant to ends and is supported by society in this, it is hardly possible to be convinced that someone else's concept of the means is relevant unless another condition for the concept of public interest is that the end justifies the means. The difficulty with this proposition, however—when it is anything more than a statement that norm X is higher on a normative scale than norm Y—is that it demands a classification of norms that does not exist, and that could not exist under Barry's conception of public interest. By adopting a relativist view Barry has made a complete end–means distinction—with all its ramifications—impossible.

The weakness of relativist statements about norms comes to the fore if one takes some specific examples of the kind that a democratic government under Barry's scheme of public interest would have to face. The public wants 'law and order'. That is the end. A policy in the public interest under Barry's view would be one which increased the opportunity for it whether the public recognized or accepted it, or not. It would be the government's duty to ignore objections to their methods. With no further restraints on its policy than 'equality of treatment', Barry's democratic government would thus be granted alarming police powers.

But even if some things the public desired gave Barry's policy-makers arbitrary powers, others would leave the government with no real—or limited—decision-making opportunities. For it is not some nebulous statement about public health and welfare that people desire but specific legislation for or against fluoridation, chlorination, sewers and so forth. If the government recognized this, it could do little else but choose between two alternatives, no matter what experts might say about what was best. On the other hand, there is nothing in Barry's idea which would prevent the government from categorizing specific desires as mistaken means toward an end and insisting that what was 'really' desired was health and welfare, the means to which lay entirely within the province of government. Theoretically, the same could be done with any of the specific public desires. On the whole, then, Barry's demythologizing of Rousseau by identifying the General Will and public interest in a way peculiar to him does not really prevent Hegelian possibilities. Under Barry's scheme it would be very easy for the state to be the arbiter of the good while professing to be thoroughly democratic.

Public Interest Norms and the Democratic Order

The need for a concept of public interest creates a difficult problem for the theorist: its norms must have general applicability or be capable of adaptation to different political orders. If we are to talk of 'government',[12] the rules enforced by the given political system must bear some relation to the problems of society as seen by that society and this would seem to imply that all governments have some notion of public interest. Yet the norms of public interest must also be specifically adapted to the democratic order, since it is this system which poses the central problem by having changed its assumptions about the source of its norms; that is, the belief that the public interest is served by respecting 'public opinion' has been replaced by the view that the task of a democratic government is to serve this interest despite pressures of public opinion. The source of norms is no longer felt to be the people, yet if the government itself—because it serves the public interest—is the source, it can hardly be called democratic. Somehow the public interest concept must incorporate democracy's two fundamental premises —egalitarianism and individualism—or the real issue has been evaded.

The requirement that public interest norms fit a general theory of government and have a particular application to democracy obviously precludes Brian Barry's attempt to make the majority into a sort of 'normative sovereign' functioning in the system of government as natural law does with Bodin, for Barry's system is exclusively democratic. There are other

[12] It seems illogical to apply the term 'government' to a system that simply enforces rules.

reasons for rejecting a concept of public interest that attempts to derive its norms from a particular system of norms: there does not seem to be any political order with a normative base broad enough to supply what is needed. Thus in a democracy there is fairly general agreement that public assistance to the needy is in the public interest; but it is obviously impossible to justify this in terms of 'equality' without implying that the present assistance is inadequate—that its inadequacy is against the public interest. In a relativist society a large number of people relate the existing assistance to public interest: they have no other norms to apply. Yet clearly the present system cannot for other reasons justify the support that public assistance to the sick, the poor, the insane and so forth receives from those who must foot the bill. Only a doctrinaire egalitarian could suppose that it would be in the public interest to enforce equality in a society which derives its drive from the absence of such a condition.

As critics of the present welfare system are likely to point out, egalitarianism is conducive to a system which virtually ensures that the recipient will be content to remain on welfare unless forced off; that is, he is told in effect that he has a right to free support as a result of some anti-egalitarian factors in the society which have interfered with his opportunities. Being on welfare can thus constitute a perfectly legitimate status in the community, and if the standard of living provided is not comfortable enough, the recipients have a 'right' to protest: the society is not fulfilling its duty. Since it is impossible for a society to make the status of welfare recipient both a right to be demanded and a reasonably comfortable one to enjoy, an egalitarian rationalized system of welfare will inevitably have standards of welfare that are always below their potential levels. If they are raised, more and more people will prefer to enjoy the advantages of the system, and the number of citizens with a sense of grievance will increase, for egalitarian-rationalized welfare is satisfactory only if it supplies a standard of living that is at least 'average'. The system is illogical and unworkable. It benefits no one to retain it—neither the general taxpayer who is faced with a constantly increasing burden; nor the state, which is threatened by an increasing body of aggrieved citizens; nor the welfare recipient who gets insufficient help.

We know of systems with a different rationale—operating in primitive communities or the family—that work quite well. The disabled members are kept in comfort so long as they need it. The sense of kinship, of oneness, that leads to this is, of course, not possible in a modern society. But it is absurd to talk of the 'selfishness' of modern society as the cause of its social ills. The democratic political order and capitalist economic system would collapse if people were not primarily 'selfish'. Nonetheless, a modern megalopolitan society is still a community of sorts and needs to be able to act as one. The problem is that we cannot expect the proper attitude from the public. Even if everyone agreed that it would be good to have a 'community spirit', no one would know how to develop it. Nor can we expect a government that follows the majority rule to promote such a spirit: adding up private wills can enable action to be taken when irreconcilable individual and group conflicts might appear to make it impossible, but it cannot deal with the problems of society as such, for the method of deciding on action poses the wrong question. The question is not what most people would want as private individuals; rather, it is what everyone would want if they were capable of thinking of themselves as members of a small community with common interests. If we assume that it is reasonable to expect a government to have a sense of community, we might define the public interest as being in part the norms of community and kinship. Because the latter are necessary to the welfare of any community but are unrealizable by the private citizen in a large community, they must be expressed by the sovereign.

The Content of Public Interest

If it is reasonable to suppose that 'public interest' refers partly to those norms of community life which are recognizable but not readily defined by members of a large community, it is not reasonable to suppose that the term is sufficiently comprehensive—just as the expression 'law and order' is not comprehensive enough to encompass the entire content of 'sovereignty'.

The concept of public interest has value because it supplements rather than replaces other norms; unfortunately it offers no clear solutions or methods. Democratic norms 'work' because they are thought to be complete in themselves. We know—more or less—what is meant when we say that all men are—or should be—equal. But what is a government supposed to do when it is told that it should act in the public interest? Even if we agree that the logical requirements of 'sovereignty' supersede those of democracy because it is a statement about government in the abstract and that the logical requirements of public interest do the same because the latter is a statement about 'community' in the abstract, the statement does not give enough 'information' to the decision-makers to make rational decisions possible. Decision-makers are faced with specific problems involving specific normative conflicts: norms of property, freedom, equality, law and order—to name only a few—enter into the simplest conflict situations. A statement about public interest may prevent a decision-maker from insisting on the inviolability of one of these norms—say, law and order—but it will not enable him to determine what policy to follow. When 'public interest' is treated as a norm with some specific content, it becomes a defence of what is otherwise not defended, the excuse a decision-maker uses when he is not sure why he has chosen a particular course of action. In this way, it tends to acquire a content in the process of being used to excuse violations of other norms. We know what our ancestors were able to do with 'nature' as a norm and what our own society can do with 'science' and we do not need another rationalization. The dilemma of public interest is not only that at present it lacks a clear content capable of guiding the formation of definite decisions, but also that it can conflict with norms which supply fairly definite goals.

Although the content of 'public interest' is hard to define, its very existence as a sort of supreme goal may prevent the actual working norms of democracy—or of any society—from becoming tyrannical rules or doctrinaire formulas of such importance to the society that they must be followed out to the letter. Since relativistic doubts about absolutes would appear to make any doctrinaire position in a relativist society impossible, such a possibility may seem remote. But the relativist's doubts are limited to the possibility of rationally analysing norms and defending them. The fact that norms express goals makes it necessary for a relativist to treat them as absolutes, for to him there is no point in changing them or debating them. He assumes that the norms of a society pose no real problem so long as they are observed; in effect he escapes the problems caused by disparate norms by denying that a problem 'should' exist. Thus if a conflict between the requirements of liberty and egalitarianism is shown to exist, the relativist will describe as the norm whatever accommodation is reached. But this is of no help where policy-making is involved: decisions have to be made when conflicts arise; and there must be a method of arbitrating conflicts between normative requirements which rests on something more than the authority to make decisions. Otherwise, arbitrary decisions will destroy the very system—if it is non-arbitrary as in the case of democracy—that allows the decision-maker to act.

No one has yet devised a system of norms which provides a clearly non-arbitrary method of solving conflicts between the norms, which by nature do not have mutually exclusive applications. To resolve tensions in non-arbitrary fashion, a concept like Hans Kelsen's supreme norm is required. Now if this norm has a definite content, its position will certainly be disputed; for although men can agree upon sets of norms, they cannot agree on their relative importance. In Kelsen's view, it should be remembered, this problem does not exist. All that is necessary is that the norm be accepted as such.

The 'supreme' norm will be accepted as such only if it is directly relevant to the issues arising out of conflicting norms and does not introduce any extraneous concepts, such as the importance of law and order. Although one might wholeheartedly agree that law and order are essential to the functioning of other social norms and are in a sense supreme, one cannot agree to avoid other issues for this reason without saying that 'law and order' is the only norm. As the only norm it would be indefensible, for it would be meaningless: law and order without laws or anything definite to keep in order. Law and order do not exist unless a super-norm in some way acknowledges the genuineness and importance of the issues between the norms in conflict. In a democracy, this means that the conflict between individualism and egalitarianism must be resolved through a concept which recognizes the dual composition of democracy's normative basis.

Chapter III

Sovereignty and the Crisis of Authority

The attack on the classical concept of sovereignty has taken many forms and appeared under various guises. One of these is a reluctance to discuss sovereignty as a valid idea and—since it is impossible to avoid it altogether—a tendency to find a substitute which sounds more acceptable to the modern ear. The concept of authority is one on which many critics of sovereignty have aligned their sights in the hope that being less 'burdened' with history and scholarship, it is more likely to serve their purpose by appealing to a wider variety of viewpoints. What meaning is attached to 'authority' and in what way is the present discussion of its 'crisis' relevant to the concept of sovereignty itself?

The Crisis of Authority

The 'crisis of authority' is an expression which a social critic is often likely to use simply because it seems a convenient way of describing the restlessness and rootlessness, relativism, and lack of clear-cut social distinctions, that are characteristic of the modern world.[1] There are some popular apprehensions that

---

[1] One thinks, for instance, of Hannah Arendt's discussion of authority which begins with a reference to the 'crisis' and its 'most significant symptom', its 'spread to such prepolitical areas as child-rearing and education' (*Between Past and Future*, The World Publishing Company, Cleveland, 1961, p 92) but ends by specifically excluding American society from the predicament. Illuminating as her discussion of Greek and Roman authority and her comments on Machiavelli are, one feels vaguely hoaxed. The phrase which at the beginning of the essay seemed to refer to democratic societies is found at the end to be a reference to the predicament of other societies. As a

may indeed be called a crisis of authority. What worries traditionalists is the problem of social order: that authority based on position in a social hierarchy, though essential to the functioning of a modern society, is undermined by attitudes to norms and authority inculcated by society. The classical argument for sovereignty is in essence an argument for the necessity of a hierarchical order; classical political philosophers considered this order so essential that the only authority they recognized was one deriving its power from a structure made legitimate by a universally recognized necessity for social order. If their argument is sound—and it would certainly seem logical and consonant with the facts of social order today—there is indeed a crisis of authority, for what we are supposed to believe about humans is incompatible with the structure of their relations. If all men 'should' be equal, the hierarchical element of our society ought not to be there. (A crisis of authority becomes inevitable, as a consequence of egalitarianism.) One ought not to defer to anyone except the 'expert', or—if a hierarchical structure is indeed necessary—only 'experts' should be members of the hierarchy.[2] This means, of course, that our method

[2] The egalitarian premise has made it possible for the social authority to seek the advice of the expert without seeming to abandon his role. In a democracy, authority is dependent on office, not the assumption that the office-holder has all the qualifications to act without recourse to others. In the courts something of the old aristocratic deference is still enforced; but even here consultations with so-called experts in human relations and psychology are becoming common before sentence is passed, and magistrates are now being selected as much for their expertise in law and psychology as for their political orthodoxy. This is what we would expect, for egalitarianism ostensibly recognizes only the authority of expertise. All others are really public servants: not to be deferred to, but commanded. Thus, not only is a democracy more open to the opinions of the expert, then, but it is virtually compelled to make its authorities 'experts' in order to retain their authority.

result, the meaning which she attaches to the 'crisis of authority' is by no means clear. A similar case is that of de Jouvenel, who in his book *Sovereignty* also refers to the 'crisis', but who must be talking about something quite different. Indeed, it is de Jouvenel's very view of the fundamental nature of authority that makes it difficult to define his opinion of what constitutes a 'crisis of authority'. It is rather odd that he should use such an expression, for it would seem that if 'authority' refers to natural deference, a crisis could never arise. It would appear that, regardless of the social structure, a fundamental type of authority would remain.

of obtaining the topmost elements of the socio-political pyramid—voting for party members—is fundamentally unsound. Those elected ought not to be elected, if they do not have the qualifications. It is not enough that we 'desire' them, assuming that we have a free choice in expressing our 'desire'. As members of a hierarchy on which depends the continuance of this freedom to choose, they must be chosen on quite different grounds; but this is not possible because of our assumptions about norms, not to mention our knowledge of human beings.

'Crisis of authority' appears to be a useful term when the authority represents either the constitution or the sovereign power. When serious and widespread doubts arise concerning the validity of the norms structurally necessary to society—the 'constitution'—or when the structure necessary to social or political authority—sovereignty—is called in question, one may speak of a crisis of authority. (Doubts about particular judicial decisions or the ability of particular office holders do not in democratic societies constitute a crisis of authority; however, in societies whose structural norms require unquestioning acceptance of those in office, they may do so.) On all other occasions we are simply looking at the doubts and indecisions, the turmoil and lack of direction that result from social change; these are recurrent phenomena in today's world.

De Jouvenel, as an astute observer of society, must be aware of this. What meaning, then, would he ascribe to 'crisis of authority'? Though his concept of authority ultimately rests on a personal relationship, he knows that authority is socially significant only when it endures; when it transcends the individual, as it were, just as society does. He suggests several techniques for maintaining the continuity of personal authority so that it will parallel the continuity of society. However, he seems well aware that these techniques cannot ensure that the authority will be transferred to a successor; and that even if it is, there is still the problem of new 'authorities' arising and challenging the legitimacy of the traditional ones. It seems that for de Jouvenel the essence of the 'crisis of authority' is this: we have not evolved a method of ensuring that the social and natural authorities coincide; there will therefore be an enduring crisis between the 'natural' authority and the one required by society.[3]

For de Jouvenel, authority is 'the faculty of gaining another man's assent' or 'the efficient cause of voluntary associations.'[4] This re-definition is important to the social sciences in general, because de Jouvenel's 'authority' is no longer primarily a juristic term applicable only to advanced, tightly organized societies: it is a 'primitive' term, a fundamental concept essential to understanding all group action. De Jouvenel is quite aware that he has given a wholly new direction to the concept and takes pains to show that he is not violating the spirit of language by using the old word 'authority' to convey the idea, which he finds implicit in the etymology. He argues that the two classical explanations of the group—'spontaneous convergence of wishes which have arisen simultaneously in the breasts of all' and 'domination'—are equally inadequate, the former violating known facts of group formation and the latter presupposing the very thing it seeks to explain.

In addition to emphasizing dynamics and making the term 'authority' available to those who have doubts about the universality of juristic conceptions, de Jouvenel's view has other advantages. He enables us to avoid a commitment to either egalitarianism or absolutism when thinking about society. A man who thinks that clubs, societies, trade unions, cartels and so forth are founded as a result of the converging wishes of those who have become members is unmistakably thinking along 'democratic' lines. A man who thinks they are forced upon members by circumstances or by another's 'power' is either a determinist or an absolutist in his thinking. There is no such commitment to established ideology in de Jouvenel's attitude.

---

[3] Hannah Arendt's meaning is more difficult to define. It is her reference to 'hierarchy' and to the spread of the 'crisis' to pedagogy which gives a clue. She appears to be thinking of the crisis that arises when a society depends on norms that make it intellectually impossible to accept an authority whose power to lead is derived from its position in a hierarchy. If the argument for sovereignty has validity, and if it is true that egalitarianism is incompatible with a social hierarchy, Arendt would say, I believe, that we are faced with a crisis of authority.

[4] Bertrand de Jouvenel, *Sovereignty: An Inquiry into the Political Good* (The University of Chicago Press, Chicago, 1963), p 29.

Apart from the philosophical, there are potentially great practical advantages to the view. We live in a world generally committed to the egalitarian philosophy, which requires that group action must arise from the 'spontaneous convergence of simultaneous wishes'. The evidence of this ever having occurred—even in small, homogeneous groups—is small. The possibility of its occurring in the heterogeneous megalopolitan states of today is practically non-existent; to act at all, egalitarian states have had to superimpose on the primitive egalitarian doctrine a 'secondary' theory which makes the ritualistic expression of 'spontaneous convergence'—voting—a temporary grant of power, a sort of recurrent creation of the sovereign. Unfortunately for social stability, the 'secondary' theory also derives whatever appeal it has from egalitarian assumptions. It simply demands a more complex process of thought. In effect egalitarian societies have split into opposing camps: simplistic thinkers who want 'the people' to decide everything, and the more reflective who recognize that nothing could be decided by the people even if they tried. The result is a form of the 'crisis of authority'.

Part of the answer to this problem can be provided by the classical theory of sovereignty which makes a statement about the nature of government that is as simple and clear as primitive egalitarian theory (unlike the higher-level 'secondary' theory of egalitarian government). However, the classical theory of sovereignty says little about the relations between individual and authority; and it is vague about the types of conflict arising from these relations and characteristic of our society. According to classical theory, doubts about particular legislation or officialdom represent indirect attacks on sovereign power. Consequently, the theory puts too much weight on what may be a minor objection and offers but one solution to doubts about authority: obey the law or else. Thus the Hobbesian social contract addresses itself to the problem of how human beings—assuming they have the nature Hobbes postulated—could acquire and accept a government and what its nature would have to be. In Hobbes' theory there is need for coercion from the very beginning, even though the initial coercion is within the individual and is that of reason. De

Jouvenel's theory is more voluntaristic. In a world where community action has been frustrated by the unrealistic requirements of egalitarian theory, de Jouvenel offers a way out—a concept that is about group action, not merely group existence.

The authority de Jouvenel discusses is a non-rational, non-normative phenomenon: men act together because a leader induces them to do so. They follow because he is the leader, and they follow the leader's successor because he derives his institutionalized authority from his predecessor's charisma. The action that results is not necessarily in the interest or according to the wishes of the followers: they do not follow out of self-interest. The leader is in effect their 'will' and decides their choices, though de Jouvenel allows the leader to adjust his imperatives to their character and inclinations,[5] so that there is room for the commonly known paradox (attributed to Alexandre Ledru-Rollin) of the leader leading by following: 'I am their leader; therefore I have to follow them.'

There is no question that this type of authority exists: the more we study group behaviour, the more we become aware of its non-rational and non-normative basis. It is not that de Jouvenel's position violates what we know about human behaviour, but that it violates what we have traditionally supposed that behaviour ought to be. He has treated as normal, behaviour that we have always considered aberrant. This in itself does not constitute a valid objection—inversions of commonly accepted views have served as illuminating ideas in history—but if one believes that rationality and normative behaviour are essential ingredients of order in a society, one must reject the view.

Why do we persist in linking reason and norms with authority? We tend to think: 'An authority is one who knows best—an expert; an authority is one whose power derives from his position in an orderly system acceptable to us because it seems a rational order in keeping with our norms.' Why do we act as though this were the case, if in reality authority has derived its power from a non-rational, non-normative relationship? We do so probably not because we have been deceived by appear-

---

[5] See: Bertrand de Jouvenel, *op cit*, p 76.

ances, but because the separation between reason and action implicit in de Jouvenel's concept of authority makes purposeful behaviour impossible. Without purpose—goals set by rationally acceptable norms—we come to feel that we are the victims of our past, a part of the chain of cause and effect which we must already have rejected if we believe in the concept of free will. But 'free will' is dependent on reason and norms, on the selection of goals other than those determined by the 'mechanical' interaction of biological self and circumstances; this interaction—if it were the sole determinant of behaviour—would unquestionably keep us within the cause-effect chain. When we talk of freedom in society, we are ultimately looking back to the concept of free will: we want what is required of us by society to be rationally acceptable to us as individuals. If it is not, we feel we are living under a tyranny, even though there is no manifest coercion.[6] We need a concept of freedom which relates freedom in society to free will. To preserve an individual's dignity as a human being, his sense of being something more than a 'thing', his relations with society must be the same as his relations with the physical world: there must be a self contemplating a not-self and capable of choosing rationally its responses to the not-self. Deny man that possibility, integrate him into a social order in a way that neither he nor anyone else understands, and he loses his freedom, for he loses his capacity even to conceive of himself, let alone make rational choices.

From this position, which may or may not be wholly normative, stems what is beyond doubt purely normative: a refusal to accept the view that a leader—having the nature attributed to him by de Jouvenel—must become detached from his followers the moment he attempts to lead. This view not merely violates the principle of the brotherhood of man; its other major weakness is that it explains only activity, not direction.

---

[6] The fact that most people support the régime under which they live may be only further proof to the freedom-lover that the régime is a tyranny, which has deprived its members of the capacity for rational understanding of what their position really is. In the last analysis, a tyranny can be defined as 'an irrational political order', whose fiats cannot be predicted and therefore cannot be taken into account in deciding our behaviour, or—if predictable—cannot be obeyed willingly because they are contrary to reason.

To lead, to decide any issue, one needs norms; but when the norms are introduced—always by the leader, of course—two types of human beings emerge: the leader and the followers. Society becomes completely dependent on the leader, not because he is at the top of a hierarchical structure, but because he is the only one who can lead. His continued existence becomes the prime concern of everybody. They must all be prepared to die for him—since there can be no certainty of a substitute being found, and because without that particular man, not just any leader, society would disintegrate. When men begin to think in this way—and they do so again and again—they ignore the lessons of history. It seems preferable to regard all particular authorities as expendable: neither worth assassinating, nor worth dying for.

Authority, Freedom and Rule-Governed Activities

In a postscript to his paper on 'Authority', Peter Winch suggests that the question to which he has addressed himself is 'What is it about human life that makes the concept of authority applicable at all?'[7] He recognizes that his answer[8] does not provide an adequate treatment of the problem of political authority, which he says 'requires an analysis not just of the way concepts in general enter into life in human societies, but of the way a particular set of political concepts enters into the life of a body politic and into the binding together of its members under a common régime.' Winch apparently supposes he failed to make the distinction clear enough and consequently implied a proposition he now rejects: 'the fact that one is a human social being, engaged in rule-governed activities and on that account

---

[7] Peter Winch, 'Authority', *Political Philosophy*, ed Anthony Quinton, p 110.
[8] The answer in brief can be found on p 100: 'All characteristically human activities involve a reference to an *established* way of doing things. The idea of such an established way of doing things in its turn presupposes that the practices and pronouncements of a certain group of people shall be authoritative in connection with the activity in question.'

able to deliberate and to choose, is in itself sufficient to commit one to the acceptance of legitimate political authority.'[9]

Given that social life involves rule-governed activity, Winch argues that 'to participate in such an activity is to accept that there is *a right and a wrong way of doing things*, and the decision as to what is right and wrong in a given case can never depend *completely* on one's own caprice.'[10] Winch differs from R S Peters—whose article on the same topic precedes his own—by insisting that the authority required is conceptual (ie making a grammatical statement) rather than contingent ('arising out of the tendency of men to come into mutual conflict').

Winch's attempt to derive *all* conceptions of authority from the notion of a 'right' way of doing things poses such serious problems that we may doubt whether *any* conception of authority has such a source. He recognizes only one of the problems involved in moving from the voluntary recognition of 'authority'—as in playing chess or learning a language—to the imposed (involuntary) authority of a parent or state, but there are other difficulties in supposing that a chess authority and a magistrate are members of the same 'class'. In addition to the involuntary element discussed by Winch, there is the fact that whereas the voluntary recognition of a chess or language 'authority' in a sense leads to one's becoming an authority oneself, nothing similar happens when we recognize the authority of the state. The expectation that such a thing could happen in the latter case is present in the projections of some anarcho-communists; but as soon as we ask what authority *is*, the parallel between political authority and expert preceptors breaks down. It also collapses when we consider the consequences of becoming an authority by recognizing authority: in certain

---

[9] *Ibid*, p 110. I suggest he did not fail to make the distinction—in fact he deliberately sought to blur the distinction between types of authority—but rather failed to see that the question he was really posing himself was that of the relationship between the concepts of authority and freedom. By addressing himself to the latter problem he has brought to light some interesting aspects of his own, as well as de Jouvenel's, concept of authority.

[10] *Ibid*, p 99.

circumstances we then cease to recognize it.¹¹ Thus the user of language who acquires confidence in himself, or the player of games who has learned the rules, may 'rightly' challenge his former preceptor, whose views become for him but opinions of no greater validity than his own. Therefore either Winch's conception of the nature of authority—even that of the chess authority—is wrong, or his conception of one kind of authority is right but it is the language which has created a false relation: it is a linguistic accident that a preceptor and a magistrate should both be called 'authorities'.

[11] Assertion: 'The consequence of becoming an authority as a result of recognizing an authority is that one ceases to recognize the authority.'

This would appear to be true only under special circumstances. When the rules are conceived of as being open to change, as they are in a political order, any particular authority other than the sovereign power must conceive of himself as subordinate to those above him in the *hierarchy*, though superior to those below him or outside the system (in the sense the public is 'outside' the state's administrative system). The appalling arrogance of minor officials in many European bureaucracies would seem to reflect this sense of authority, which is so contrary to the democratic spirit that strongly egalitarian societies such as the USA have avoided emphasizing hierarchical relations of power at the expense of efficiency. Civil servants in the USA and Canada are prone to show a great deal more initiative and independence of judgement than their European counterparts, mainly because they do not conceive of themselves as 'authorities' at all. They think of their work as a job requiring the solution of problems, rather than as a set of rules to be applied.

However, under circumstances where the rules are regarded as *not being open to change*—that is, where all behaviour is conceived of as being subject to rules which, as in chess, have been prescribed once and for all—accepting an authority means the same as 'learning the rules', which when once learnt put one on the same level as any other 'authority'. Such an 'authority' is not part of an hierarchical system. He and others like him are part of a primitive egalitarian system typical of small tribal organization. Once the rules have been learnt one is as much an authority as one's mentor, who, of course, ceases to be mentor or 'authority'. When this occurs is not easy to decide, so that primitive peoples using the system make much of coming-of-age ceremonies which are arbitrary points in one's life when one becomes an authority to those who have not undergone the rites and achieves equality of authority with those one formerly recognized as authorities. Because our society is 'democratic' and recognizes an egalitarian norm, one is likely to confuse these two kinds of authority. (Democracy is being considered 'natural'—accepted by even the most primitive tribes—and the notion of a sovereign power is being rejected.) To some it has always seemed more 'democratic' to advocate a system of rules which all can learn and which—having been learnt—make one 'equal' with the others who have learnt them.

Winch's argument that freedom of choice, 'rules' and 'authority' are inter-related, rests on the view that in order to conduct any activity—from scientific experimentation to playing football—one must make certain assumptions and establish arbitrary rules of procedure. Because of this fundamental resemblance we can speak of the 'science of football' or the 'game of logic'. Winch, following Wittgenstein, analyses 'freedom', 'rules' and 'authority' in terms of the game metaphor. He implies that in accepting arbitrary rules we must be recognizing some authority, even though it might be difficult to indicate just who it is. The fundamental difficulty with this view seems to lie in the link which Winch attempts to establish between freedom of choice and rule-authority.

Following de Jouvenel (in particular, his statement: 'To follow an authority is a voluntary act. Authority ends where voluntary assent ends.') Winch argues that authority is a precondition of liberty: 'To be able to choose is to be able to consider reasons for and against ... Reasons are intelligible only in the context of the rules governing the kind of activity in which one is participating. Only human beings are capable of participating in rule-governed activities, hence other animals cannot be said to deliberate and choose.'[12]

Now we can agree that 'choice' requires rules: that is, we can so define choice as to deny that animals are capable of it. True choice, we might argue—although Winch does not develop the point—requires us to follow certain rules of procedure that enable us to take into account the consequences of acts not yet undertaken and compare each act and its consequences with certain arbitrary standards—and on this basis decide what action to take. Because the mere possibility of an alternative course of action does not constitute choice, we can define the rules of reason as necessary to choice and hence to freedom. But Winch violates one of these rules of reason by assuming that since the rules of reason necessary to choice are arbitrary, arbitrary rules are necessary to choice: he merges all sets of rules into one identity on the ground that their fundamental assumptions are arbitrary. However, the point is that, arbitrary or not,

---

[12] *Ibid*, p 102.

the rules derive their meaning from the activity they permit—and the activity differs for each set of rules. Thus the rules of reason give rise to freedom of choice; but the rules of tennis give rise to tennis. Rules may be of one kind in the sense of being ultimately arbitrary, but they are not all of one kind in their consequences, as regards the activity they permit. If we agree that we achieve freedom of choice through rules of reason, we cannot agree that parental rules about being home at midnight or pedestrian traffic rules that we do not cross on a red light achieve the same effect.[13] Mere taboos and arbitrary fiats do not entail freedom of choice; nor are they intended to. If rules did not differ in kind, we could transpose a set of rules from one activity to another or engage in all activities by applying a single rule—the fallacy of the 'good'. But if they differ in kind, the authority conceptually linked with rules must also differ in kind. The authority of an expert chess-player cannot be the same as the authority held by the president of a republic. The alleged relationship between 'freedom', 'rules', and 'authority' is not proven by Winch's argument. What does emerge, however, is that there is an indefinite number of authorities—all differing in kind—and that only one of them—reason—gives rise to freedom.

Another weakness in Winch's view is due, I believe, to his failure to recognize that in accepting an authority two quite different acts occur: acceptance of a rule or rules, and acceptance of some person who has a special relation to rules and hence to those who obey them. The acceptance of rules, however, does not imply acceptance of an authority unless one of the rules is that such an authority shall exist. In fact, the very act of accepting rules—rather than accepting an authority—makes each person his own authority, so that he acquires the right to question the claims of another who professes to have a

---

[13] Winch's argument that parental authority over children does not encroach on freedom because it serves to induct them into modes of social life is specious. The aim of parents is to inculcate certain rules so that they will always be observed and so that the possibility of their being broken or even questioned will not arise. Only if another rule ('meta-rule'?) is also inculcated—the rule that accepted modes of behaviour must be questioned—can the existence of rules permit freedom.

special relation to rules. This is one of the major problems of democracy, which begins with rules rather than authority. It is also a major problem advanced by Winch.

Authority and Political Obligation

The 'rules of the game' of the Hegelian state make the latter the source of norms; in a democracy the same role is ascribed to the individual. Theoretically, each system would 'work'—there would be no conflict of authority—if the rules represented a genuine assumption about all norms—if every member of the state were properly 'socialized'. In practice, however, both systems raise the issue of obligation, because no process of socialization can eliminate the distinction between the norms of the individual and those of the state. For this reason the rationale of both systems attempts to eliminate the distinction: the Hegelian doctrine denies that the individual can exist apart from the state, while the democratic system asserts that the state cannot exist apart from its members; each approach tries to simplify the problem of authority by denying the existence of the situation that gives rise to it. But if 'authority' is to mean something more than 'power'—ability to impose norms—its definition must specify the relationship between the individual's and the state's norms. This cannot be an arbitrary rule of the game: it must take cognizance of the fundamental distinction between the state and the individual.

Obligation—which makes no sense outside a normative context—is not easily accepted by a relativist society. The behaviouralist, of course, regards the question as idle. Confronted with the fact that most people obey authorities most of the time, he studies the techniques of socialization, coercion, and legitimization that produce this result. Confronted with the converse that some people do not obey authorities, he studies the aberrant situation. Again he has no use for political obligation: thus obedience and disaffection are for him unrelated phenomena. The relativistically-inclined theorist also tends to dismiss the question. If he sees all norms as expressions of individual tastes and desires, legal norms must partake of their nature, and as such represent the desires of most members of the society. Under this view no problem of obligation arises: as with behaviouralism, we are confronted only with a fact. This result is inevitable, for relativism sees norms as being of one type only—expressions of desires or social conventions—whereas the question of obligation arises from the assumption that two kinds of norms are equally valid: those of individual conscience and those of the state, specifically those enforced by law.

In this setting 'government' is in a special position—it is a sort of force that arose in response to a situation. As it must follow a certain policy, it must have a set of norms, but it does not itself constitute an ideal norm: it is more like a 'conscience'. In the latter capacity, it tries to solve problems created by the individual's recognition of what he believes in—his norms—and by the individual's recognition of his existence in society.

In other words, when we refer to 'authority' we are speaking of the norms of the private individual versus those of the individual-in-society—a system in which authority is vested in the decision-maker, the government, which is not itself the supreme norm. Thus it is not true that we must obey the law because it is the supreme norm. We should follow the dictates of the law for the same reason, and with similar reservations, that we follow the dictates of conscience. The law can be compared with the conscience of the individual-in-society. If we suspect it has been motivated by the government's self-interest, the law has no more claim on us than the dictates of a private conscience motivated by self-interest. 'Authority' viewed in such a way enables us to avoid splitting our personalities and deciding issues according to claims of public and private interest.

The problem with the 'obligation' concept is that its proponents tend to misunderstand the question at issue. They want to move somehow from the norm of private conscience to that of the supremacy of law—to pretend that we must either accept all the decrees of a legally constituted authority or revert to the Hobbesian state of nature, whereas the real problem is to decide at what point the authority must take precedence.

Theorists often discuss 'obligation' purely in terms of authority rather than the norms which legitimize the authority. Such an approach invites the conclusion that a duly constituted government, recognized by its citizens as legitimate, can pass and enforce any law consistent with the norms establishing it. If this were not so, 'authority' would be meaningless. But this view also entails recognition of the dangers inherent in the supremacy of legally constituted authorities and its advocates always make a prior case for the necessity of democracy. They argue that—since the elective system imposes a restraint on potential tyranny—government is always aware that it will be called to account at the next election; until then, however, it must be free to act according to its lights. This approach contributes a simple definition of 'authority': that which must receive habitual obedience. But it ignores the fact that we do resist some of the decrees of authorities recognized by us as legitimate. In consequence, 'authority' tends to be redefined to mean 'holding coercive power'—a departure from the original definition. Thus simplification of the problem of 'obligation' also simplifies the 'authority' concept, with the result that neither deals with the question of obedience, or reflects our attitude to both authority and law.

Sovereign Authority and Sovereign Law

The assertion that the law must be obeyed is often identified with the assertion that in every state there must be a sovereign authority, or is at least made a corollary of the theory of sovereignty. However, a little reflection shows that this view is narrowly juristic and incompatible with the classical conception. Hobbes himself allowed for resistance to the law which did not constitute a denial of the principle of sovereignty.

The argument that the concept of authority requires us to obey the law—authority being first defined as that which must be obeyed—and that such authority is necessary to social order—authority now being defined as that which needs to be obeyed—attempts to reduce the question of authority to a simple confrontation between order and anarchy. The rational man is presumably expected to prefer order and by his choice give the authority he recognizes power to coerce his irrational fellow man. Such a simplification of the concept of authority ignores the real problem, which is that a rational man who begins with the premise that order is preferable to anarchy can nonetheless legitimately resist some decrees of an authority he otherwise recognizes; in effect, he denies that an authority is that which always is, or must be, obeyed. Hobbes had the rational man do this when his own life was threatened, a view which seems to me to mistake the very logic of sovereignty. The problem of authority and sovereign power is not that of deciding when a particular kind of self-interest should overrule the general self-interest that establishes sovereignty. A single exception based on self-interest provides an argument that destroys sovereignty as a normative system. The moment we talk about norms, as we necessarily do when we talk about sovereign authority, we must observe the basic normative law that we cannot make an exception of the self. To do so is to deny that we are talking about norms we recognize. If the question of authority is seen as representing in any way, at any time, an opposition between self and sovereign, the sovereign is effectively denied the kind of authority essential to his existence. If obedience had to be coerced, as it would be where a conflict of interest between self and sovereign was possible, the sovereign would lack the power to coerce which comes from the fact that he is obeyed.

The view that the law must always be obeyed would produce such a situation. In effect it is a denial of the classical concept of sovereignty: that is, it substitutes sovereignty of the law for sovereignty and in so doing undermines the argument for sovereignty as applied to the law. Kelsen's argument for this legal sovereignty is that there must be a norm of norms, so that conflicts about norms can be settled. Obviously, if this norm of norms is that the law must be obeyed, it cannot serve its function of settling conflicts within the system. By professing to see the problem of authority as the problem of anarchy versus order, then, we create anarchy by destroying the ordering principle. 'The law must be obeyed' says nothing about conflicts over the nature of laws themselves.

A similar situation arises when we attempt to view the problem of political authority as one of obeying or not obeying the law: when, in effect, we pretend that acceptance of the concept of an ultimate decision-maker is the same as accepting the proposition that the law must always be obeyed since the law represents the command of the decision-maker. The alternatives here, too, are represented as anarchy and authority. But this is not the problem as most of us see it. The problem is what to do when a conflict arises between what the state says must be done and what our conscience says should be done; this will occur frequently in a political order such as democracy, which recognizes the validity of the individual's norms as well as those of the state. We cannot say that the law must always be obeyed without denying the premise about the validity of private conscience. We simply ignore the problem by so doing and give an interpretation to sovereignty that for most members of a democracy would effectively destroy their sense of obligation. A state in which the sovereign's decision always invalidated the claims of conscience would not be democratic and hence for the democrat would have no claim at all upon him: the sovereign power would invalidate its claim to sovereignty and would thus promote anarchy. Those who argue for the authority of the law overlook the fact that acceptance of the decision of an ultimate decision-maker is not the same as saying that the law of the state must always override the claims of conscience. The sovereign is not the law and must not be identified with it. He is 'above' the law in the classical conception, which is another way of saying that the sovereign—as well as subordinate authorities in the system—does not and must not take sides in conflicts between the norms of the individual and those prescribed by the state. If he did, no one with respect for the individual would submit to the jurisdiction of the state. The phenomenon of those who are opposed to certain laws submitting the question of their resistance to the courts would not occur and every question of conscience would become an issue of anarchy versus order. Because too many in authority view the question of authority in this way, there has been a drift toward an anarchistic outlook among members of the public; the latter have been forced to view the question this way and have naturally preferred their own norms to those of others. Thus, a fear of anarchy can create the very conditions it fears. Not until we can trust the sovereign authority to be absolutely impartial in regard to disputes between normative orders can we overcome the problem of civil disorder we ourselves create by misunderstanding the nature of sovereignty.

The misconception of sovereignty which we find among members of the judiciary, who above all others ought to have a clear conception of the role assigned them by the theory, is not necessarily the result of simplistic thinking on their part. Rather, the traditional democratic 'solution' to the existence of the two authorities or sets of norms invites the view that the law must always be obeyed. The democratic view has long been that the law in a democracy incorporates the conscience of the individual through the process of continuous legislation or at least incorporates those aspects of private conscience which the nature of life in society permits. Those who oppose the claims of conscience to the dictates of law are illogically repudiating the claims of other people's conscience and endangering the one type of society which gives substantial recognition to private conscience.

This view of the nature of authority in a democracy is still put forward by theorists, although it makes the concept of legal authority applicable only to democratic societies. The argument suggests that in non-democratic societies the law would not be felt to be binding, would not in fact be legal. It has other weaknesses: it equates justice and law in a way acceptable only to a relativist and in so doing equates the General Will with the will of all, this in turn with the will of the majority, this again with the viewpoints of those who obtain office through the elective process and this in turn with the legislation passed. If we suspect—and nothing else is necessary—that the chain of equations has a weak link, the argument for authority of the law is worthless. No one could feel 'bound' by such a chain.

The most important objection to this view of authority, however, is that it entails repudiation of the logic of classical sovereignty and acceptance of the impossible view that those who submit to authority are somehow themselves the authority to which they submit. Thus if 'authority' is over coercive, it is so only towards minorities. For everyone else it is consensual, which here means 'a matter of common agreement about norms'. Now if we are to talk about political realities, the one thing we cannot do is to begin with an assumption about normative agreements. If we could postulate that, we could dispense with government, which is made necessary even in primitive groups by the presence of unavoidable normative conflict. Such conflict is inevitable because even where there is assurance about the content of the normative code, in regard to any one individual, there can be no assurance about its application in particular situations. Knowing that individuals are often unable to make choices because of normative conflicts within themselves, we can hardly postulate a society where all or the majority can somehow make those choices and, having done so, come to an agreement that they will not insist on their choice if most other members of the community insist on theirs. Relativists imagine that we can, because for them there is no real reason why anyone should insist on his normative position. Given that view, it seems perfectly plausible that a society could agree upon an 'authority' which would supply the goals and make the choices that would otherwise not be possible. Where the 'authority' would get its own norms is not considered. The chief weakness of the view, however, is that it does not describe any known or conceivable society: norms thought to be pure conventions—or the result of a pure convention—would lose their binding power, so that the 'authority' set up by the kind of 'agreement' that results from indifference to alternatives would have to become purely coercive. As such, it would be incapable of being coercive at all, since coercive power—other than the physical superiority of one man over another—requires cooperative effort.

The relativist assumption about initial agreement has plausibility only because some sort of initial agreement about what constitutes a legitimate government is necessary; but such an agreement is possible only if it is recognized as not being an agreement about a normative order or an authority which can countermand the norms of others. In a democracy we might well agree that a government shall be arrived at by majority rule, but this is not the same as saying that we have agreed to the overriding authority of the majority rule principle—we may well refuse to be relativists, and find it impossible to believe that people can rule themselves. What we have accepted is government and a method of arriving at one. To accept the former, we have to feel assured that it will indeed be a government, and not a tyrant: that it will never claim that the norms of society have precedence over those of the individual. Should a dispute arise about any particular law or policy, justice must prevail: that is, we must be able to feel that the sovereign power in such a dispute will not take sides and destroy its sovereignty by identifying itself with any one element in society or any party to the dispute. Under the sovereignty concept, the law is not the sovereign authority.

Is 'Authority' a Substitute for 'Sovereignty'?

It would seem at first glance that 'authority' says all that 'sovereignty' does, while escaping major difficulties: in particular, that it enables a primary and persistent misconception about sovereignty to be avoided.

Repeatedly, commentators have supposed that sovereignty is an argument for government by the arbitrary will of one man or body—an argument for absolutism—and that the obvious fact that a single will does not prevail in any state is clear evidence of a serious defect in the logic of sovereignty. Decision-making, they point out, is an extremely complicated process. There is, of course, no evidence that Bodin or Hobbes ever thought otherwise. They simply were not interested in how particular decisions are reached; their sole aim was to demonstrate that without a supreme decision-maker there will be neither a complicated nor a simple decision-making process, and that any infringement on his decision-making powers is an infringement on decision-making itself. A system of checks merely prevents recommendations from being carried out. It is not arbitrary power that is checked, but power itself, for under the concept of sovereignty, arbitrariness comes from below, not from above: it is the mistaken substitution of the private will of functionaries in the decision-making process for a rational analysis of what the situation demands. The mistake made by the commentators is that they suppose sovereignty to be simply a method of placing someone at the top of a hierarchical power structure—that it is a description of a purely static phenomenon. But this is not the case. It is above all else a description of a process of decision-making. It does not presume that decisions represent only the will of the top member of the hierarchy. The decisions at the top depend almost entirely on those below, just as the power of the sovereign depends on the structure, rather than on his own physical strength. It is rather bewildering that although everyone recognizes that the power of the sovereign depends on those below him, so many nonetheless suppose that the will of the sovereign is in some way completely independent of the structure.

Like sovereignty, the concept of authority entails some sense of legitimacy, so that it defines a normal social relationship—unlike coercive power concepts, which apply to exceptional conditions. Although it is less open to the charge of 'absolutism', to which the concept of sovereignty is more vulnerable, 'authority' can refer to so many different phenomena—from the psychological phenomenon of Weber's charismatic authority to the legal phenomenon of constitutional authority—that it suffers from the same multiplicity of meanings. However, unlike sovereignty, 'authority' seems incapable of integrating its diverse applications: thus, although external and internal sovereignty can be shown to be logically related, charismatic authority and legal authority would seem irreconcilable, held together only by the idea that each is regarded as in some way legitimate.

However, to substitute a concept like 'supreme authority' for 'sovereignty' may not be without merit. Its advantage is that it describes a legal-psychological phenomenon without introducing the concept of state; it can be understood purely in terms of the community. The concept of sovereignty, on the other hand, demands a concept of the state as distinct from the community. Whereas 'authority' is entirely meaningful as a statement about relations between individuals, sovereignty is not, unless we reduce its meaning to 'dominance'—a reduction that completely changes the meaning.

'Authority' or 'supreme authority' are also attractive as substitutes for 'sovereignty' to those who regard the state as an orderly hierarchy of rules observed by its members. In such a system there is a logical need for a supreme authority, a point beyond which a dispute cannot be carried, so that all disputes are settled because they cannot be continued. This 'supreme authority' may be a constitution or the community itself—the people—so that the concept of supreme authority as a substitute for sovereignty has the advantage of fitting neatly into a democratic framework in a way that sovereignty does not.

Attractive as all this may seem, it finds no recommendation with the political scientist who finds merit in the very intractability of sovereignty—its refusal to lend itself readily to any particular ideological order, while making a statement of universal applicability.

But perhaps the crucial argument, for the political scientist, against using authority as a substitute for sovereignty is that it embodies a purely juristic—and therefore static—conception of the state. The jurist is quite right to postulate a supreme authority in his legal order: such an authority is logically necessary. But in the mind of a political scientist a legal order presupposes a working political order, which needs a sovereign not bound by the supreme legal authority. Laws do not cover every conceivable situation, they do not apply of their own volition, nor do they have any bearing upon the initiation of action. The law says only that certain behaviour is not legitimate; it prevents rather than initiates action; therefore, only if we regard the state as a static phenomenon can 'supreme authority' be supposed to convey all that is inherent in sovereignty.

Chapter IV

Sovereignty in Political Theory

Sovereignty has many meanings in political theory.[1] The principal traditional division in meaning—and therefore an essential issue in political theory—has been that of political *versus* legal sovereignty. The main characteristic of legal sovereignty is that it takes law—which is in fact a part of the concept of sovereignty and a consequence of a system of sovereignty—and attempts to make it the system itself; it imposes itself upon the community and somehow 'gathers' the power to do so during the process. The concept of legal sovereignty suffers the defect of presupposing a basic stability in social relations—a stability that would make the very concept of sovereignty unnecessary. Legal sovereignty has become closely linked with the 'democratic' view of sovereignty, even though its requirements are such that 'democracy' becomes essentially a description of a ceremonious induction of a government into office at more or less regular intervals.

The Nature of Sovereignty

Classical, political 'Hobbesian' sovereignty, unlike its legal counterpart, does not assume that in order to have its essential characteristics authority must be imposed. In this respect, political sovereignty fulfills the requirements of democratic theory, but it differs from the latter in an important way: it

---

[1] Among the many 'types' of sovereignty which have emerged in political theory are: political and legal, internal and external, *de jure* and *de facto*, influential, limited ('semi-sovereignty'), relative etc.

recognizes that life in society requires a set of norms that cannot be assumed to be a part of man's nature—the laws of society can never simply reflect the will of the people, no matter what may be the form of government. Ultimately, a good part of the authority of the Hobbesian sovereign rests upon the individual's recognition that his (the individual's) impulses and interests are not social in any meaningful sense but private (even when he is sociable and gregarious) and that to require him to take an interest in the kind of decisions necessary is unreasonable, even if one can assume he has the qualities necessary for making 'right' decisions. Hobbesian sovereignty creates the conditions which are needed for such an interest to exist. Democratic theory, attempting to assign ultimate authority to the 'people', has not been able to overcome the problem of public and private norms. In order to mediate between the two sets of norms, it is inclined to adopt legal sovereignty which means abandoning the norms of individuality for the norms of the 'constitution' and insisting that everyone adapt his behaviour to a static conception of society while living in one that is unmistakably changing.

In estimating the real significance of sovereignty in relation to other concepts of authority the following is important: the strength of an authority within its jurisdiction depends on the genuineness of the 'contract', the presence of 'consent', the degree of 'obligation' felt, or however we want to express the relation between the government and the governed. In the Hobbesian concept, 'consent', 'obligation' and 'contract' rest on a measure of reflection, a consideration of alternatives: 'sovereignty' will not exist at all among those incapable of the effort required. The consequence of the rational element in the Hobbesian contract is that society must value reason, or the sovereign power will be much weakened. (The contract is not a historical fact but a condition of life in society.) The significance of the theory of sovereignty, when we consider the alternatives, is that it makes no attempt to replace what is in fact the supreme norm—the individual's conception of his own worth—by some other norm seemingly more adapted to life in society. It does not presuppose an authority in order to argue that such authority must be powerless, or that some other authority or power must prevail. One's own sense of supreme worth and importance—on which the contract ultimately rests—remains in force, as indeed it logically must.

To speak of 'entities' in which, according to various theories, sovereignty does or should reside, provides a short-cut to the ideas of particular thinkers. They simplify the categorization of theories according to the 'locus' of sovereignty: the monarchy (the person of the monarch, according to Bodin; the monarch or his assembly, according to Hobbes); the people (Rousseau's sovereignty of the General Will); Parliament (Austin); parliamentary and judicial institutions (Dicey's political and legal sovereignty); shifting 'pluralist' groups (Laski). A commonly held position is that the locus of sovereignty is important because it determines the relationship of the individual to the state and government. In fact, sovereignty *itself* states that relationship. That is what sovereignty is about.

Locating sovereignty in the people, the constitution, or the various institutions violates the logic of the concept: such plausibility as is possible is achieved by isolating concepts of 'power' and 'authority' from all other considerations. It is important to the concept of sovereignty *not* to give it a locus. 'Where ought the sovereign power of the state to reside?' asked Aristotle, 'With the people? With the propertied classes? With the good? With one man, the best of all the good? With one man, the tyrant? There are objections to all these.'[2]

In studying the question of the locus of sovereignty it is easy to assume that where there is influence there cannot be sovereignty, since sovereign power is supposed to be *indivisible*. Since even absolute monarchs had their advisers, who sometimes made all policy, some critics argue that the lack of locus is proof of the non-existence of sovereignty in the sense required by the theory. Their arguments, however, are based on a different idea of 'power' than that applicable to the sovereignty theory; their conception is defined by mechanistic theory and ultimately by pre-Humean definitions of causation which implied that the connection between cause and effect is necessary as is the case with logical relationships. (Hume denied this;

---

[2] Aristotle, *The Politics* (Penguin, Harmondsworth, 1964), p 121.

furthermore, to him causal inference was not experientially certifiable.) In fact, the 'power' of the sovereign is not the power of being uninfluenced. Sovereignty is not a simple embodiment of power; nor is it a statement about supreme power alone.[3] The system is not mechanical, with a prime mover at the top, paralleling medieval theological views of God's relation to the universe. That is where critics of sovereignty like Laski went wrong.

Historically, the question of the locus of sovereignty has been important to political theory because it unites various objections to, and re-interpretations of, sovereignty. The inability to locate in *any* society a sovereign power having the attributes held to be necessary in *all* societies has led to interpretations that either assign a location to the sovereign or make the question meaningless. By making the locus coextensive with society, modern thought makes locus meaningless with regard to *internal* sovereignty: nowadays, the 'constitution' is not a written document having a location but the normative set of a society; the 'people' of popular sovereignty theory are not merely the majority who vote a government into office but all adult members of the state.

Perhaps the most misunderstood attribute of sovereignty concerns its so-called 'unlimited' character. Among limiting factors, natural and positive law, the constitution, conventions, and 'practical' limitations are usually mentioned. Objections raised against sovereignty imply that they are 'limitations' on sovereignty, whereas in fact they are denials of the latter. Instead of clarifying the subject, they explain the concept away. By being labelled 'unlimited', 'omnipotent' etc sovereignty is transformed into a shibboleth: an old-fashioned, abandoned doctrine. Pronouncements by critics have obscured the original meaning: the definitions of the 'classics' are often quoted, but neither their assumptions nor the implications of their ideas (or their relevance) are adequately considered. Thus to dwell exclusively on the oft-quoted definition by Bodin 'Majestas est summa in cives ac subditos legibusque soluta

---

[3] On the relation between 'power' and 'sovereignty' see the Introduction to my symposium *In Defense of Sovereignty* (Oxford University Press, New York, 1969), especially pp 9 ff.

potestas' ('highest power over citizens and subjects, unrestrained by laws') and to play down Bodin's qualifications (that the sovereign is limited by natural and divine laws and by the laws of the realm) is to miss the intent of the doctrine, which was to make the sovereign non-absolute. Similarly, a standard position is that Hobbes' argument has no room for either natural or positive law limitations on the sovereign power: it is argued that according to the nature of the system, the sovereign as supreme legislator and as judge responsible for the enforcement of his law cannot be made subject to it; and since the law thereby made is the only kind one can be subject to (= that can be enforced), the sovereign is not subject to natural law, even if it exists. The ugly thought that the sovereign can do absolutely anything has made people feel that they do not want such sovereign power and inclined them towards a political order that satisfies the requirements of the argument for 'sovereignty' while escaping the 'problems of absolutism'. The usual solution—as advocated by the jurists—has been to make law the sovereign power. But law itself cannot, of course, be that. It is true that it can set up a system which fulfills the most necessary conditions of government. Thus the American Constitution describes what may happen if a particular law is enforced; yet, probably most of those interested in having a particular law come into force know that the Constitution will not be of any real help. Decisions are not made according to the 'plan' described in the Constitution, although the latter is supposed to be 'sovereign'. Law runs counter to the logic of sovereignty, notably by failing to supply the ultimate decision-maker capable of commanding because he can exact obedience.

How the Hobbesian sovereign came to be regarded as capable of commanding anything he wishes is hard to determine. It could not have come from Hobbes, who made it clear that the sovereign cannot violate the logic of contract—the desire for self-preservation which continually renews the contract for each of us born into a society having a working government. A sovereign power that could do absolutely anything—for instance, destroy at random the members of the state—would not be acting as a sovereign power, which must act in a particular way in order to be defined as such. (The Hobbesian sovereign is not unlimited, because a truly unlimited sovereign power cannot be accepted as sovereign by its subjects and hence cannot be sovereign.) The 'omnipotence' of the sovereign differs from the omnipotence of God who (according to most theologians) can violate his own laws and reverse or cancel them. While omnipotence is God's attribute, the 'omnipotence' of the sovereign power cannot exist and be defined independently of sovereignty—this is why we do not speak of sovereign omnipotence.

How then to resolve the dilemma of sovereignty's 'unlimited' nature? The problem is that one seeks the impossible—a system of norms as binding on the sovereign as statute law is binding on his subjects. If we think of 'limitation' from a legal point of view, the sovereign is beyond question unlimited. But the advocates of theories of sovereignty must believe in some limitations on sovereignty, since the concept is based on normative preference. The system must have room for the norms it is designed to protect. This would not be possible if the sovereign were 'unlimited'. Because the sovereign must perform his functions in order to remain a sovereign, pure relativism is excluded as a basis of policy. One must not try to impose any limitations on sovereignty by some other power with higher authority. The logic of the sovereignty of God excludes the sovereignty of the Prince, since the requirements of divine law would sometimes make the Prince a criminal and an outlaw and as such unable to sustain his claims to authority. Sovereignty cannot permit normative objections of that order to be raised. If the Prince, like any other man, were no more than a subject of the Divine Sovereign, divine law would be a denial of the Prince's sovereignty. The 'social contract' would be with God, not men, and revolution would be inherent in the system. But the characteristic of sovereignty as a logical order is that it has no place for revolution. The notion that 'rebellion against tyrants is obedience to God' does not describe anything possible under the logic of sovereignty: not because sovereignty excludes the concept of tyranny but because it makes 'tyranny' a type of incompetence rather than evil-doing. A true tyrant is unable to command obedience: revolution is obviated by the system. The concept of divine law, however, with its implicit concept of a Sovereign God, makes tyranny an evidence of illegitimacy and therefore invites revolution. If sovereignty is to be limited by divine law, the latter must be seen as coextensive with natural law, which is law not because it is the product of divine fiat but of divine reason, in which man himself can participate. Natural law or 'normative assumptions' serve as limitations on sovereign power by forming a normative framework in which the system operates. It is absurd to represent sovereignty as a system which begins with norms but ends with normless anarchy.

A Re-wording of the Classical Definition of Sovereignty

The classical definitions of sovereignty—that 'absolute and perpetual power over citizens and subjects in a Commonweale' (Bodin)[4]—and of the sovereign—'the mortall God' who 'may use the strength and means of them all [members of the commonwealth] as he shall think expedient, for their Peace and Common Defence' (Hobbes)[5]—are clear enough within their contexts. Yet the emphasis on 'power' and the unlimited sovereign will, which broke with the Christian tradition of the Prince as the embodiment of justice and is incompatible with our own predilection for the rule of law and the constitutional state, arouses a hostility that blinds many to what is being said. Repeatedly, the classical viewpoint is identified with 'supreme power', unattached to any function, as if Hobbes and Bodin were more interested in defending special privilege than in preserving order and good government. It should be clear, however, from the Hobbes quotation given above and from Bodin's discussion of the sovereign function, that sovereignty is not a statement about 'power' but about government and the state, and that the power referred to derives from the function it serves.

[4] Jean Bodin, *The Six Bookes of a Commonweale*, ed K D McRae (Harvard University Press, Cambridge, 1962), Book 1, Chapter VIII, p 84.

[5] Thomas Hobbes, *Leviathan* (Dent, London, 1965), Chapter XVII, p 90.

To avoid unnecessary misunderstanding of the classical definitions, we might substitute 'decision-maker' for 'power', and incorporate the function of the sovereign into the definition. We might also take cognizance of F H Hinsley's[6] contribution: thus, sovereignty refers to the necessary presence in any political order incorporating heterogeneous elements, themselves capable of exercising power, of an ultimate decision-maker whose decisions relating to his function are recognized as binding and/or can be enforced.

The meaning of 'necessary' here depends on the validity of the classical arguments, which can be reduced to the proposition that social order cannot be maintained when interests conflict, unless someone has the means ('authority' and/or coercive power) to resolve the conflict. The type of society is specified in the new definition because it is possible under certain circumstances, described by Hinsley, for a society to be organized other than in terms of sovereignty. It does not appear possible, however, for any present-day state to be so organized, so that if it is understood that the concept of sovereignty is applicable only to what we know as the state and its relations with like units, then the qualification can be omitted. 'Ultimate' has been substituted for 'supreme' or 'absolute' in the hope of avoiding the common, but quite uninformed, objection that in no society does anyone or any group make all decision free from the influence of others. Both Bodin and Hobbes explicitly repudiate the view that the sovereign makes all decisions without being influenced by others or by social circumstances—to suppose that he could is simply absurd—but there seems to be something in the words 'supreme' and 'absolute' that encourages the absurdity, so that it is better to avoid them. 'Decision-maker', too, has been substituted in order to avoid unnecessary confusion. Despite the fact that the classical statements quite clearly reveal that 'power', because it derives from the sovereign function, incorporates all species of power (authority, coercive power and influence), the use of 'power' in the definition of sovereignty remains a source of confusion. The substitution of 'decision-maker' should also make it clear that the classical statements relate to the dynamics of political organization,

[6] F H Hinsley, *Sovereignty* (Basic Books, New York, 1966).

not its formal constitution. A 'constitution' cannot be sovereign. Finally, the decisions that are binding and enforceable have been limited to those 'relating to his function', because it is the function that enables them to be binding and enforceable.

The Significance of Sovereignty [7]

The importance of the 'neo-classical' concept of sovereignty is that it is firstly, a logical formulation and secondly, a tool of analysis [8] and a unifying formula, capable of integrating a number of political concepts.

Sovereignty today is not only a fact of social order but a logical necessity. It is a fact of political life, in that despite all the criticism directed against the concept, the present-day exercise of sovereignty is not far from the tenets of the classical theory: the sovereign tends to be an 'unlimited', supreme coercive force which expresses itself through legislation. Furthermore, the loss of support for values in general has once again made order the central value, as it was for Bodin and Hobbes. Sovereignty makes a logical statement—a statement which depends on its logic and not on the accuracy with which it describes political conditions. It is a declaration that if order is to have certain characteristics, then an ordering body or sovereign having certain qualities must exist. It is precisely these attributes that make the concept important to both citizen and government.

Being directed towards the individual citizen, the classical argument was—and is—a statement about obligation and body politic. It is also a counterstatement to unrestrained egalitarianism, which is based on literal equality. Unlike sovereignty—which requires a clear-cut distinction between community and state—egalitarian theory demands an identification: it considers the state a fiction. But literal equality is no longer acceptable. Egalitarian slogans only promote the modern malaise, the

---

[7] The argument in this section is taken from the conclusions 'The Validity of Sovereignty' in my symposium *In Defense of Sovereignty* (Oxford University Press, New York, 1969), pp 291 ff.

[8] To be discussed in a separate section.

rebellion of disassociation—the feeling that although the government is legitimate, its practices are not (because it is not acting as the agent of the majority), so that it can be ignored whenever one can do so with impunity. The citizen denies that he has duties or obligations to a government which does not behave as it 'should'. Abandoning his role as citizen, he pursues narrow self-interest and the government is left without the direction or controls necessary to its functioning. If the theory of sovereignty could replace the slogans of primitive egalitarianism, much could be done to restore the sense of community so badly lacking in our society: it would be realized that we have a common set of principles, and that it is the government's function to uphold and implement them, and act in accordance with them.

As to members of the government, they are left at the moment without a clear statement of the nature of their function. Traditional democratic statements are not very helpful: they do not solve the conflict between the desire to carry out the wishes of the electors and the desire to serve the 'public interest'. Consequently, members of the government regard frequent departures from democratic requirements as expedients which must be concealed. The result is intellectual and verbal dishonesty and the frequent use of clichés and empty phrases by democratic politicians.

Without a clear conception of sovereignty (and its requirements) the sovereign body in a democracy has no principles of action. How should a government act when it is not acting in accordance with majority will? If public interest requires that the public will be occasionally ignored, on what basis is one to arrive at a concept of public interest? It is sovereignty that can provide such a basis. Without the latter only two courses are open: response to circumstances without reference to principles, or the avoidance of action whose course is not clearly indicated by circumstances. The first produces indecision and a lack of coherent policy; the second, a reaction to political and social crises which takes the form of 'brinkmanship'.

Sovereignty and the Public Interest

If sovereignty is important to the concept of public interest, so is public interest to sovereignty. The theory of sovereignty defines sovereign power in terms of a function performed. That function can be described as keeping 'law and order', but such a formulation has led to false inferences as to the nature of sovereignty, namely that the acceptance of sovereignty is tantamount to the acceptance of any law whatsoever. Classical analysis of sovereignty would reject such a position as false. The coercive capacity of the Hobbesian sovereign depends on the public's sense of obligation to maintain conditions superior to the (lawless) state of nature. Just what precisely these conditions are is clear neither to the sovereign nor to his subjects. To refer to these conditions as the 'public interest' would not necessarily mean that a new meaning has been injected into the theory of sovereignty. The 'public interest' is the jurist's 'law and order'. The newer term helps avoid the juristic tendency to assume that the 'contract' has led to a transfer of 'authority' which makes the individual agree to submit his self-interest and private conscience to the authority of the sovereign whose only obvious qualification is superior coercive power. The subject has in his conscience an authority which can lead him to resist the sovereign's coercive power; hence the sovereign needs a counteracting 'authority' in addition to his coercive power. In other words, the concept of 'public interest' is important to 'sovereignty' because it expresses the kind of sovereign 'authority' which would parallel the subject's authority.

Whereas the concept of sovereignty defines 'law' as the will of the sovereign, it does not define 'public interest' as sovereign's action. But this is not a disadvantage. 'Law' as the command of the sovereign promotes an illusory notion of the nature of government—the fallacy that legislation alone can solve the problems of society and that a 'good' society is noted for the number and ferocity of its laws. Identification of 'public interest' with the sovereign's acts rather than his norms—as would happen if sovereignty defined public interest—would lead to a parallel view. Thus, a further advantage of replacing the term 'law and order' with 'public interest' is that it makes it hard to confuse sovereignty with absolutism.

The relationship between the theory of sovereignty and the concept of public interest is not free from complications. The sovereign authority derives its power from and acts according to a 'public interest' theory which is linked with a private interest theory of human behavior. Thus in Hobbes' view, human behaviour is 'normative': we order our wants in terms of our awareness that the immediate impulse is not the only one we have or will have. Individual desires become relativist norms. By nature they are in conflict and man, seeing no other way out, consents to a power whose interest is to maintain such conditions in society that each man can follow his own principles within the limits the sovereign power permits. (In the Hobbesian analysis, no private individual has any sense of public interest—which has awkward consequences for the sovereign, since his private interest lies in maintaining the public interest.) To what principles does the sovereign look in order to fulfill his function as sovereign and thus retain power? The Hobbesian sovereign is no jurist who can suppose that the mere enforcement of 'law' would satisfy the requirements of the contract, for his power derives from other people's self-interest. Clearly, there could be many occasions when the sovereign, acting without a clear notion of the public's self-interest, would violate so many private interests that the sense of obligation would disappear and sovereignty would be lost. Hobbes himself gave the problem a deceptive simplicity by pretending that the alternative to the acceptance of the sovereign power is a return to the state of nature. It is clear that the sovereign without an adequate sense of the 'public interest' is threatened more by a transference of sovereignty to another than by a readiness on anyone's part to do without government.

There is also the problem of defining the nature of public interest. The necessity for doing this becomes obvious if one considers the consequences of abandoning the concept. On the one hand, one can postulate a government's will which is in every respect like the sovereign will except for the absence of 'public interest'; in this way one achieves in effect a sovereign power without a supporting theory of sovereignty. Alternatively—following the relativist denial that human behaviour is normative—one can see government as a locus of forces acting upon society. According to the latter view, agents react to circumstances which society confronts; everything is determined by antecedents; no one wills anything. Determinism (implicit in relativism which identifies norms with wishes) is thus brought to the fore when relativistic analysis is applied to the study of government. What would be helpful in this connection would be to analyse the consequences of identification of norms with private desires.

'Government' does not make sense when defined in terms of the wants of those composing it. Both the power it possesses and the obedience it exacts become inexplicable when so defined, and the policies followed by most governments bear so little resemblance to what we would expect from private individuals wielding power and pursuing only their own interests that some other explanation of their policies is necessary. Sovereignty is of course a general theory of government whose requirements are necessarily modified by the actual types of government. Thus the Hobbesian contract is not meant to be a description of how government attains power but only how it retains power. Democratic ideology, on the other hand, apart from supplying an operating method for attaining a government, also offers statements—often conflicting with the theory of sovereignty—about how a government should govern. Democratic government is frequently represented as carrying out the desires of the majority (modified by 'rights' assigned to all) so that in effect 'public interest' is often defined as precisely this type of behaviour on the part of government. But it is not possible for the will of the majority to be the will of the government or for the government to define 'public interest' in this way. Indeed, the 'democratic' definition of 'public interest' itself becomes a problem for government. The nature of the democratic process of attaining government strongly tempts its members to do just what a large portion of the public expects, though their own familiarity with the art of government suggests the need for some other concept. (One of the main problems in government is the allocation of resources, but the will of the majority cannot be employed as a basis for allocation, because the average man does not have sufficient knowledge of the relevant factors: to give only two examples, he does not know with any precision what resources are available, or the comparative social returns to be obtained from applying them to alternative uses.)

Sovereignty as a Tool of Analysis

Although sovereignty has been used by various authors with reference to the 'state', 'authority', 'law', 'obligation', 'power', 'government', 'legitimacy' and 'constitution', not much has been done to bring together the various views and to use the concept for the purpose of ordering and defining terms which at present conflict and overlap. The most obvious reason for this is that most discussions are defences of, or attacks upon, the concept rather than attempts to use it, and those theorists who do employ it are generally interested in a related concept rather than in sovereignty itself: that is, they find it necessary to define some concept that seems more immediately relevant, such as 'law' or 'authority'. The difficulty has been that if one author finds the concept necessary to (say) a definition of the state, another can attack his approach on those very grounds. He can argue that there is something wrong with a definition that requires us to postulate another concept which is primarily a logical requirement of a system of ideas rather than an observable 'fact'. This is not the way science is supposed to work. Political scientists, like all social scientists, are acutely embarrassed by the lack of a unifying theory and by the impossibility of finding one by generalizing from descriptions of types of behaviour which are recognized as unique. Some other factor is clearly involved here and this would seem to result from the combination of democratic predilections with a relativist bias, unlikely as that may sound.

The problem with sovereignty throughout its history has been the difficulties it raises in regard to democratic theory: acceptance of the one raises grave doubts about the validity of the other. Even a cursory reading of the literature reveals that most attacks on the concept of sovereignty are based on its 'undemocratic' implications. No true relativist, of course, would make such an attack. However, according to relativists, in a society which happens to be democratic, it is the fact of democracy that is important, not because it is by nature more important than sovereignty, but because society makes it more important by regarding it as such. Thus the theorist who opposes scientism on the grounds that the norms which man sets for himself and the beliefs he acts by are the true determinants of behaviour, however 'unreal' they may be, is confronted with an opponent who can accept his approach but deny that he is talking about anything significant in most societies today. The relativist might be perfectly willing to discuss society in terms of sovereignty provided the system were in force, but since (in his view) it is not, sovereignty is irrelevant. It seems to me that the only way to remove the impasse is to show that because sovereignty permits a definition of terms and an integration of norms such as 'law', 'government' and 'authority', we do in fact, even in a democracy, meet the logical requirements of sovereignty in preference to those of democracy: we recognize them as the basis of social order. When a whole-hearted democrat says that the law must be obeyed, he is certainly not talking about a democratic norm, even though theorists have naturally attempted to integrate this attitude into democracy; whether he has heard of the concept or not, he is thinking in terms of the requirements of sovereignty. So, too, with the other terms that sovereignty enables us to define. Consequently, the failure to use sovereignty as a tool of analysis is simply a failure to recognize the norms that society—any society—is in fact using. In the thinking and behaviour of most men, the fundamental concepts of 'law' and 'order' take precedence.

With or without the concept of sovereignty, the political theorist is confronted with a number of terms, such as 'authority', 'power' and 'obligation', which have long been used outside his field. It is the theorist's task, of course, to decide the extent, if any, to which they apply within his field. Now, without the concept of sovereignty, these terms will be defined—or, if one wishes, the type of behaviour to be studied will be classified—in accordance with the circumstances obtaining in quite different areas of personal relations: that is, without the concept of sovercignty, the political analyst investigates the validity of drawing an analogy between the state-society relationship and father-family, priest-congregation, mob leader-mob relationships, and so forth. It is not that analysts are so naïve as to suppose that the relationships are the same, but rather that the concepts have to come from somewhere (behaviour does not classify itself) and without sovereignty to supply the concept, the source must be situations which appear in some degree analogous to the state-society relationship. The rejection of sovereignty as a tool of analysis, then, implies either that the analogies are valid and we can understand political phenomena by understanding personal relations, or that the concepts which sovereignty defines are not relevant to political analysis. Since it is not possible to select areas for investigation without concepts that show them to be of one type, we must conclude that guiding the analysis of those, such as the behaviouralists, who reject sovereignty are assumptions based on analogies that if given explicit statement would be rejected as unsound. The principal characteristic of sovereignty as a tool of analysis, in other words, is that it begins with a logical requirement posed by a general situation—namely, that there shall be an accepted method of settling conflict among groups—and hence supplies concepts which may or may not be analogous to those used in other situations; the latter is a matter for sociological analysis.

It might be felt that behaviouralistic analysis of the concepts not defined by sovereignty could modify them to suit the empirical difference between (for example) the authority of a back-bench politician and that of the same man when holding office, but in such situations, it is still the analogy which supplies the definition of 'authority'. One is compelled either to find a similarity underlying the seeming difference, or frankly to admit the difference and hope that close study of situations showing the difference will lead to a way of conceptualizing it. The first course results in the kind of studies that strive to obscure the differences between relations in an unorganized group and those in a political order; the second leads to the mass of behaviouralist studies of what, speaking generally, happened at a particular place at a particular time. Very different as the results may be, the two approaches are in principle the same. Even though the behaviouralist rejects the analogy (unless the evidence establishes that the situations are the same) it nonetheless selects for him the situation to be investigated and the kind of evidence he will regard as relevant. Whether he acknowledges it or not, he has used the analogy by the very act of questioning it: the most that can come out of his study will be the acceptance or rejection of this particular analogy. On the other hand, those who begin with the conceptual tools supplied by sovereignty are in no way restricted to analogies between what happens in a political order and what happens in personal relations. Such analysts are quite free to establish, if they can, that political authority has no connection with personal authority. They are never driven to the behaviouralist absurdity that since certain concepts important to theory, such as that of the state, are almost impossible to define empirically, they therefore do not exist. Nor do they fall into the error promoted by relativism that any set of norms will serve as the basis of a political order provided they are accepted: these are the rules of the game-obligation-authority fallacy. For those theorists who acknowledge the argument for sovereignty, the rules of the game theory is an unacceptable analogy because relations in a political order logically require a special set of rules and hence a special definition of authority. Just 'any' rules will not do.

However, essential as sovereignty would seem to be as a source of conceptual tools that are uncontaminated by implicit analogies, great care needs to be used in employing them. It must be remembered that sovereignty itself cannot be the sole source of the definitions, since sovereignty is not a complete statement of the relationship between government and society. It says something very important about the nature of government and its relation to society, but it says nothing at all about how that government came into being. Statements about how governments are created, however, cannot be excluded from analyses of the meaning of authority and obligation. Thus it is completely unrealistic to argue that since the logic of sovereignty requires an ultimate decision-maker whose authority is final and binding, therefore all members of a society which obtains a government through the majority vote of enfranchized adults must obey. It is unrealistic because the logic behind the method of arriving at the government denies that the ultimate decision-maker has that kind of authority. Indeed, this logic asserts that those who made him the decision-maker have the ultimate authority and that as a theory about government, needed to complete the theory of sovereignty in a particular society, it has a valid claim to be taken into account in any statement about the nature of authority in that society.[9]

Numerous societies today embody two conflicting statements about authority and the theorist cannot escape the problem by expressing a preference for one or the other (the governed or the government). Since each statement about these authorities depends ultimately upon a normative statement, it is possible that no absolute statement can be made and that the most we can hope for in reducing the disorder that must ensue when a decision about the ultimate authority is not possible, is to set forth as many situations as possible where there can be no real question about who is the ultimate decision-maker. We have already taken some steps in this direction: paradoxically, by recognizing the claims of sovereignty. Sovereignty has certainly operated throughout the history of modern democracy, but past insistence on the 'sovereignty of the people', which is a denial of the classical concept, has certainly led to completely unnecessary opposition to lawful government and deliberate acts of civil disobedience. Much civil disorder today is not so much a rebellion against authority as it is an assertion of what is thought to be the only possible source of authority vis-à-vis the usurping power of 'big government'. Only widespread information about the theory of sovereignty—which must be taught together with the democratic norms—can hope to reduce this.

[9] Sovereignty makes a complete statement about authority only when we are talking about government in the abstract. An understanding of this point provides the answer to those objections to the theory of sovereignty which describe it as an absolutist doctrine. It is absolutist only in an absolutist society. Elsewhere, the statement that it makes about authority must be modified by the norms which establish the government. For this reason, it is inadvisable to attempt to 'de-absolutize' sovereignty by identifying the sovereign with the constitution. Even if there were no logical objections to such identification, acceptance of it would ensure the kind of absolutism that opponents fear.

Legitimacy and Sovereignty

'Legitimacy' has been used in three senses, with reference to: firstly, the existence of social power; secondly, the attainment of power; thirdly, the way power is exercised. In each case, 'legitimacy' ostensibly changes the fact of power; the 'must' of obedience becomes an 'ought'. As a result, 'power' reputedly changes to 'authority'.

If it were not for the evidence of history, it would be difficult to believe that the concept of legitimacy has ever been applied to those holding power, irrespective of how that power was attained or exercised. The very idea is puzzling because this type of 'legitimacy' does not seem to make sense. Nonetheless, without some such idea it is difficult to account for tyrannies. One is prone to forget that the tyrant, though defined as illegitimate in one or both of the other possible senses of legitimacy, must in some sense be 'legitimate' (pseudo-legitimate) if he is powerful enough to be a tyrant. 'Power' without 'authority' does not make sense politically: there has to be some form of authority, of directed cooperation, to achieve the concentration of power which permits the tyrant to enforce his decrees.

Behaviouralist analyses of legitimacy are frequently concerned with the first sense of the concept. S M Lipset, for instance, when he says that 'a crisis of legitimacy is a crisis of change'[10] seems to be arguing purely in terms of 'power': one faction wishes to hold on to its power and the other wishes to gain it. He uses the concept of 'legitimacy' as a mere technique of defending power or claims to power and hence deprives it of any real content. Unless we suppose that somehow 'having power' or 'claiming power' is equated with being legitimate, Lipset's discussion does not make sense.

The second concept of legitimacy—which defines an authority as legitimate if the method of attaining power is 'legitimate'—is often discussed, especially by those who use the 'rules of the game' approach to society. The importance of this concept of legitimacy derives from the fact that it introduces an element necessary to the concept of government—an orderly

[10] S M Lipset, *Political Man* (Doubleday, Garden City, 1963), p 65.

succession to power. Without it one can have *a* government, but not government, not an undisputed succession of governments. However, this concept of 'legitimacy' does not sufficiently define government, since it says nothing about the policy pursued by the government which must consist of something more than the mere issuance of fiats. Perhaps true 'crises of legitimacy', Lipset notwithstanding, are mainly related to conflicts between the two necessary concepts of legitimacy (the 'second' and the 'third')—'necessary' because they are needed to define government. Behaviouralists, who emphasize the 'rules of the game' approach, fail to understand this. They pretend that we do not really need a government, but because we play the game of politics we need rules of procedure (how to begin is one of them).

There is no need to argue that we need government and that no one will play a game which has no purpose. The concept which supplies the purpose—and also eliminates the view that the second concept of legitimacy can be regarded as a 'rule of the game'—is that of sovereignty. Sovereignty by itself is an abstract statement about the nature of government. To become an actual description, it must be related to a particular system—using the two concepts of legitimacy which define how a government attains and exercises power.

The conclusion that the advent of 'sovereignty' has reduced the meaning of 'legitimacy' to two senses may trouble the semanticist, but we should remember that the term is used to refer to a conceptual requirement, not an observable condition. We need a term which covers the two conceptually necessary conditions for 'government', because the political scientist must be able to distinguish between a 'government' and a 'régime' (a term we might well substitute for 'tyranny', traditionally used to describe 'illegitimate government'). The twofold meaning of 'legitimacy' enables us to talk about the actual methods of instituting a sovereign power as well as the policy pursued by that power, without being forced to take a normative stand. It is essential that we have a term which describes regular (as opposed to irregular) succession to sovereignty. If we deny this, we are bound to view the 'social contract' as an historical event which has somehow persuaded all posterity to accept its conditions. Or, if we want to substitute 'rules of the game' for the same basic idea, we must pretend that circumstances compel us to continue practices, even though they may be objectionable. By referring to the methods of succession, the term 'legitimacy' enables us to recognize that if it is true that the logic of sovereignty supplies a general attitude to government, an actual government having the characteristics demanded by sovereignty can be continued only in certain ways—by some technique of the inheritance of power or by some method of appointment. These are the only 'legitimate' ways because they are the only methods of maintaining a regular succession of sovereign powers—the actual government. Government—which requires a regular system of succession—cannot, strictly speaking, be usurped; it is the usurpation of power which is possible. We call the régime instituted by a usurper illegitimate, even when it is benevolent, because it violates a condition necessary for government. We can also call a régime attained by a regular system of succession illegitimate, if it fails to 'govern' effectively.

Taken by itself, the concept of sovereignty has tended to promote the notion that any and all laws of the sovereign are 'legitimate' if the sovereign power is considered 'legitimate'; the latter is either a term for the logic of sovereignty—a sort of seal of approval set on its cogency—or it is a more complex term, namely an approval coupled with the view that sovereign power has been established in a regular fashion. Accordingly, so long as laws are being made and enforced—it is argued—the government is 'legitimate'. But this is an unacceptable definition of government and legitimacy, for it disregards purposefulness in law. Under this conception, the sovereign power is seen as an autocracy which, incomprehensibly, is accepted as such by society. It denies to the sovereign any function other than maintenance of the law, while illogically granting him the power to violate it. Obviously, we need a term to distinguish between such a condition and the condition of 'government', in which the laws of sovereign power are not designed to gratify private tastes and wishes, but to serve a social function. Only such laws are 'legitimate'.

We cannot resolve disputes between those who regard as

legitimate any law passed by a sovereign power which is established legitimately and those who believe that some of the laws may be in some other sense 'illegitimate'; there is no theory which relates the two conceptions of legitimacy to each other. But there is an obvious relationship between sovereignty and legitimacy. The attempt to eliminate legitimacy by making all sovereign acts legitimate goes against the logic of sovereignty, which is based on order and requires a supreme decision-maker. Sovereignty demands the concept of legitimacy and legitimacy requires sovereignty. Neither can be understood if it is identified with, or treated as being in conflict with, the other.

Sovereignty as a Datum in International Relations

Despite determined opposition, the concept of sovereignty has on the whole endured without major modification since it was first formulated. This has been due to the logic of its assertion of what is necessary within a state. The case is different, however, with regard to relations between states. The sovereignty concept makes no statement concerning the logical requirements of international relations.

One can try to derive a logical statement by applying to states the social contract argument advanced by Hobbes: to nations are attributed the characteristics of Hobbesian individuals. In regard to each other, nations are in a state of nature; a social contract between nations, and world government, are inevitable. Such an argument, however, serves no real purpose, because there is no necessary connection between the state of nature and government. In fact, Hobbes gave no timetable for the change from a state of nature to government, nor did he make the former a necessary pre-condition of the latter.

Jurists, who require a concept of international law—but have no clear way of defining it in the absence of a sovereign power—have been in the forefront of attempts to apply the sovereignty concept to the international sphere or have argued, as an alternative, for the creation of a supra-national sovereign power. It is more than a coincidence that twice in this century representatives of states have somehow fulfilled the Hobbesian social contract hypothesis and that two major powers—first Great Britain and then the USA—have played the role of international policeman. There is good reason to suppose that the very costly League of Nations and United Nations organizations represent honest attempts to impose a world order and that talk of 'world policemen' is not a rationalization of imperialist adventures but reflects a rational appraisal of what is necessary to world order and the rule of law. If this is so, one can only be saddened by general misconceptions of the nature of sovereignty and the law.

In an age when natural law in the traditional sense was conceivable, the concept of a super-state was appropriate. The natural law concept made state law an aberration, to be one day replaced by the universally applicable natural law. Today, because of relativism, this dream has become implausible to most people; any appeal that the concept of a universal state or 'policeman' may have, is based on order alone: imposed arrangements are regarded as superior to agreed arrangements.

There is much to be said for such a view: the permanence yet flexibility of imposed arrangements make a strong appeal to many. But it is obvious that in a democracy the preference for a command régime over that resulting from agreement has a precarious basis; it is upheld primarily by those who have attained a status recognized as superior by their society: the preference will change as the status changes. It could not be validly asserted that men always and everywhere prefer command to agreement, or that they should.

Logically, the 'policeman' concept without sovereign power is impossible. Police power derives from the sovereign, not from side-arms. If men have been ready to accept the fiction of a state acting as world-policeman, it is because they thought in terms of the only institutionalized system of order they know—state law. It may or may not be necessary to postulate an extension of the sovereign power as a prerequisite to extension of the law and creation of a world-system. There is good reason to suppose such an extension would not prove feasible. If at one time it seemed easy to believe that the law of one's country should be world law, it is equally common today for men to feel that the application of national law should be restricted—that the nation should be sub-divided.[11] Traditional territorial limitations on sovereign power and ideological uniformities are felt to be less important than cultural differences: French v English; Scots v English; Walloons v Flemish and so forth.

Arguments for sovereignty on the international scale are thus out of place, since we are further than ever from the concept of universal law that would make them relevant. Without a belief in a universal law, we cannot accept the notion of a supra-national sovereign to solve problems of international lawlessness.

On the other hand, we cannot accept the view that the existence of state sovereignty creates international lawlessness, the view which—reversing Hobbes' theory—would have it that acceptance of the state sovereignty concept produces a (Hobbesian) state of nature among nations. (Sovereignty in fact does the opposite: it precludes a relapse into the state of nature.) In order to maintain that it does (create lawlessness), we should give more attention to Hobbes' analysis of personality attributes. We might notice then that in many respects nations seem to fit Hobbes' analysis of human character better than human beings themselves. Hobbes' utterly unsocial, self-centered and self-seeking individual is a more adequate description of nations than of individuals; so that if there is a relation between character and the state of nature and if part of character is the restless seeking for 'power after power', international relations must be imbued with the same spirit. However, there are some basic differences between nations and individuals. The most important is the variation in power. The Hobbesian state of nature exists because of the limited physical inequality of men: one man may be able to cow another, but there is an obvious limit to superiority in human physical strength. This is not true of the strength of the state: a single state superior in military strength to all others combined is quite conceivable.

In view of this—and assuming a state of nature in inter-

[11] Relativism, as we might expect, is coming to play a larger and larger part in the exercise of sovereignty, see section *below*.

national affairs—one is bound to ask why a monolithic worldstate has not yet come. Why should not coercive power alone have achieved an organized community life: a bully could force another to act with him and the two together could compel another until all mankind was subjected to one omnipotent bully. The reason why such a development is impossible is clear: coercive power, unlike contractual power, is not cumulative. A coercive empire holding sway over the entire earth is no stronger than the power it derives from its source— the homeland—where a genuine system of sovereign power must be operating. In employing that sovereignty for the purpose of coercion, those who attempt to extend its domain—and deny its premises, as it were—find that they cannot go beyond a certain point, at which over-extension becomes undesirable. Theorists investigating the problem find that they cannot supply a much-needed formula referring to a necessary balance between sovereign authority and sovereign coercion. But one thing is certain: over-extension of sovereignty leads to a crisis of authority in the most basic sense, by threatening the foundations of the sovereignty system.

An interesting accommodation to the absence of sovereignty on an international level is provided by the concept of the balance of power (or equality of interest). In contrast to the 'world policeman' fiction, the balance of power concept recognizes that, in default of a sovereign power, the pretence that it exists, or the attempt to create it, produces more disorder than it eliminates. (As a principle of order, sovereignty must always be more than an aspiration: it must be a fact.) Although there have been no attempts to use the balance of power concept as the basis for a theory of international order paralleling sovereignty, it has been accepted as a working principle in international relations.

It is its relationship to sovereignty which gives a clue as to why the balance of power principle continues to be accepted despite its serious deficiencies. Thus, it is not a means of taking action or of settling disputes but of preventing marked changes in the relations between states, even though these may be inevitable as the result of internal changes. The balance of *power* principle works because of the peculiar sense sovereignty gives to the concept of 'power'. It is paradoxical that if a sovereign state is to have desirable power in the sense of 'controlling', it must have power in the sense of 'governing', which can be highly undesirable. Thus many parts of the British Empire were a serious financial burden on Britain, which carried it (among other reasons) in order to exclude other nations from certain strategic territories. The burden was assumed as one of the conditions for maintaining the balance of power and was given up willingly when maintenance of the balance was no longer Britain's responsibility. The awkward fact that sovereignty can make the territorial expansion of sovereignty a doubtful advantage to a sovereign state enables international relations to show considerably more harmony and order than one would expect from the assertion that nations are in a state of nature in regard to one another. They are not in such a state: the existence of state sovereignty demolishes the basis of the hypothetical state of nature, for the ceaseless hunger for 'power after power' is then eliminated and necessary restraints imposed.[12]

The Exercise of Sovereignty and Relativism

Relativism is coming to play a larger and larger part in the exercise of sovereign power. State law is being increasingly recognized as a set of norms adapted to particular conditions: some historical and cultural, some geographic. Made necessary by the working democratic order, relativism has gone far to discredit the universalistic view—the oneness of man and natural law—as opposed to the sovereign state, which at one time was commonly regarded as an inherently 'unnatural' unit.

---

[12] The case of the Soviet occupation of Czechoslovakia in 1968 also provides an illustration: *control* by an external Communist government became impossible without direct *governing*. To achieve it meant a coercive coup and a violation of Czechoslovak sovereignty. The fact that the USSR behaved in this way does not invalidate the argument that sovereign states and the state of nature are incompatible: it is totalitarian states which through aggression change the meaning of sovereignty—and upset international equilibrium—by divesting a victim-state of its sovereignty.

Today, justice requires the breaking up of empires and the subdivision of formerly sovereign states. No one seems disturbed by the arbitrary division of states along parallels: North and South Korea; North and South Vietnam etc. At one time such divisions would have been the epitome of cynical international power politics, violations of international law because they were violations of sovereignty. Most people, however, see these fragmentations as territorial changes that violate little more than customary arrangements and which, by sharing spheres of influence, reduce conflicts between larger powers.

Some modern practices do not resemble the dismemberment of sovereign states and their incorporation into other states such as occurred in the past. The new type of division, as advocated by the new movements toward independence of people who historically have never been independent—for example, Quebec—is in keeping with the relativist view of the nature of law. Given relativism, one can no longer defend the large territorial units of today where separatist movements exist. Arguments against such movements must take the form of practical arguments emphasizing their economic non-viability, as well as the security and administrative problems which would result from separation. Arguments based on the requirements of the principle of sovereignty simply do not appear sound. Only if separatists were attempting to set up a rival government coextensive in space with the existing sovereign power would it be logical to invoke the principle of sovereignty. (There does not appear to be anything in the sovereignty principle which requires the sovereign power to assert that its territory must remain unchanged, except when claims are made by other states.)

Chapter V

Natural Law

'If I say to someone, "You acted wrongly in stealing that money", I am not stating anything more than if I had simply said, "You stole that money". In adding that this action is wrong I am not making any further statement about it. I am simply evincing my moral disapproval of it. It is as if I had said, "You stole that money", in a peculiar tone of horror...' This early statement by Ayer[1] could at one time or another have been made by Russell, Wittgenstein or Carnap. It derives from Ayer's view that a meaningful sentence must be a tautology or empirically verifiable. Since ethical terms cannot be the subject of analysis, Ayer concludes that they are 'pseudo-concepts', 'emotive' expressions which are either a simple description of the speaker's feelings or an attempt to induce others to feel as he does.

'A Peculiar Tone of Horror'

To Ayer, the assertion that 'stealing is wrong' is tautologous. His statement may easily appear correct: intuitively it seems a tautology. But Ayer's implicit line of thought—that both elements are expressions of a peculiar tone of horror—seems also incorrect. They are certainly not interchangeable, and though other ethical terms can replace 'stealing' in this construction, they cannot replace each other, as they would have to if each simply implied a peculiar tone of horror; that is, we make very clear distinctions between stealing, adultery, cruelty

[1] Alfred Jules Ayer, *Language, Truth and Logic* (Dover Publications, New York, 1952), p 107.

and not brushing one's teeth after every meal. They are clearly more than expressions of peculiar tones of horror. Ayer's mistake lies in his virtually ignoring the concept which evokes the supposed emotion.

'Stealing is wrong', is, of course, a statement about the concept of property ownership. Without that concept we might well suppose that the only reason anyone admits that stealing is wrong is that it actually does arouse the tone of horror. Presumably, there have been people at various times in various places who greeted the same type of behaviour with a peculiar tone of approval. Unfortunately for the logical positivist this is not so. It is true that there have been, and still are, societies with a sense of ownership quite different from that found in our own society. But there is not one society known where a word translatable as 'stealing' and a word translatable as 'right' are associated.

One might suppose that given the concept of property and a logical positivist value sense, other value terms logically related to property would follow: gratitude, generosity, extravagance, miserliness, inheritance and so forth. But it does not seem possible to take up a position toward these concepts—and values. The relativists' inability to explain adequately or even sufficiently consider the groupings of values is their major failure. If relativists are right in assuming that the analysis of values is complete when the latter are declared to be tastes, wishes or attitudes, it would seem impossible for moral statements to form any kind of pattern for either the individual or society. Just as it is impossible to say whether a man who likes spinach also likes ice-cream or baseball, it should be impossible to guess whether an egalitarian society or individual also believes in public education, majority rule, tolerance and so forth. In fact, of course, we do find patterns of moral behaviour which cannot be explained by the relativist interpretation. It is true that in small, closely-knit cultures where differing patterns of behaviour and belief as well as the opportunity for them are absent, the relativist position is plausible. *The Republic* does not really refute even the extremist position of Thrasymachus. Relativism, indeed, gives a plausible account of how values are held and spread by most people under most circumstances. It is, in fact, primarily a theory of communication rather than a theory of values. But the existence of patterns in a multi-cultured, mobile modern society suggests that there is a very strong rational element in values that the relativist has ignored.

Relativism begets a primitive individualism which breaks down the only justification of democracy which remains for those who reject most democratic premises: namely, that democracy is the only system which has been able to eliminate the age-long conflict between state and citizen without victimizing the citizen and making the state a tyranny. Even for those who support it (though denying its premises), democracy is not the best conceivable system of government; but at present it is a tolerable one. If relativism gains the ascendancy, it will not remain so. When members of the government and the governed both come to feel that all values, including those that form the basis of the political order, have no real binding force, self-interest can be the only guiding principle. We could argue that everybody has always pursued self-interest. But value orders which transcend the individual enlarge the self, so that each individual regards himself as much more than a creature with biological drives and purely private interests calling for satisfaction. Value orders insist on man's inevitable association with other men, and on his being more than a biological unit. Remove the values and the Hobbesian hypothetic state of nature based on a primitive egoism becomes a 'fact' of social life. Under such circumstances, it is in the interest ('self-interest') of the government and also its duty (here meaning 'function') to enforce order and insist upon the exercise of force as a value; members of the society, most of whom are aware that their very existence requires a social order, will also agree that the exercise of power by the government is good. Under relativism, then, power or force becomes a value, which men suppose is capable not only of maintaining such order as exists, but also of begetting change. When action is desired and the government does not take it, the public assumes that the former needs a greater grant of power, with the result that the traditional restraints on government are eroded. It is a pity that this should occur, for the power to act is not inevitably followed by action: there is no logical relationship at all between the two. The relativist interpretation of values seems to imply otherwise.

The Persistence of Natural Law

To the relativist, criticisms of his point of view appear to be no more than reflections of critics' prejudices. The relativist sees himself as trying to describe man's value orders without going beyond the evidence of empirical observation; he sees his critics as insisting that he does so for no better reason than that one of their desires, masquerading as a fact about the universe, is for a rational order for value statements which, in his view, because they are emotive, do not have any rational order. This places critics in an awkward position which is made even more difficult when we recognize that the 'human nature' on which natural law theorists have based much of their criticism of relativism, does not seem to exist apart from the cultures in which men develop, each of which clearly differs from the other. Even if there were such a thing as a homo sapiens— the hypothetical biological being untouched by society, the 'natural' or feral man of mythology—his hypothetical common nature arising from his biological inheritance would not be likely to produce anything which we normally call values. Indeed, man's biological drives are usually sharply distinguished from his values by most moral absolutists.

Despite serious difficulties, the tradition of natural law persists and in recent decades has become stronger. In larger part, no doubt, this is a reaction to relativism which, whether the relativist likes it or not, entails what is itself a moral position. (Because of the very nature of ethics all human behaviour is comprehended by it and any assertion about morality represents a moral position.) The relativist's notion of values implies that they are not binding and that no distinction need be made between impulses and long-range goals, between one's private interests and the demands of one's society. In effect, relativism constitutes not only a natural law for its adherents, but the whole of natural law. As such, it is open to very serious objections.

The relativist identification of values and desires denies the significance of man's experience with time. If the relativist is correct, the impulse of the moment has as great a claim as any other desire ('value'). Yet much ethical analysis—especially that relating to hedonism—has focused on man's consciousness of time; it has pointed out that whatever the nature of the happiness for which we strive, this cannot be achieved if we suppose there is no real basis for choice between immediate and long-range goals. The normal human being's experience with time, his awareness that the immediate situation will not persist indefinitely, clearly has played a very large part in his awareness that there is a difference between values and desires. Indeed, it seems to be one of the principal reasons why we make a distinction and partly explains the persistent sense that values are binding, so that we are obligated to fulfill them, even though they often conflict with our own desires. Values are to some extent desires which take time into account and hence bind us; they *are* our interests or desires insofar as we are conscious of our position in time. It seems no accident that those whom we call morally irresponsible seem to have a poorly developed sense of that position and of the need to take account of the future—they live from day to day, or from moment to moment. Adherents of natural law would say that since a sense of time appears inescapable for humans, including those who neglect it when making their choices, it clearly ought to play a part in the formulation of whatever constitutes natural law.

Relativism, Reason and Natural Law

One of the vexations suffered by those who support natural law, and have traditionally emphasized reason, is that their relativist opponents can use the tools of reason, logic, mathematics and linguistic analysis to make a seemingly invincible case for the absence of reason from ethical propositions. The relativists' fundamental propositions appear irrefutable. We cannot deny that ethical judgements ultimately rest on assertions that are not verifiable within the system of such judgements and are not meaningful outside the system. Goedel's theorem and linguistic analysis would seem to block the path of anyone who seeks to discover natural laws. There cannot be any, if our normative assumptions are all arbitrary and incapable of proof. If man can attribute normative value to any proposition whatsoever—as would seem possible if the fundamental propositions were arbitrary—it follows that reasoning about values is rationalization and the search for a set of natural laws illusory. Ethical judgements must then be identified with the non-rational elements in man's character and culture: his tastes, wishes, customs and so forth.

But the logic of relativism leads to a major difficulty—the identification of sets of phenomena which are empirically distinct (no satisfactory explanation of this distinction being supplied). We call something a value rather than a taste or custom when it is felt to be universal—limited in application, if at all, only by some other value of a similar nature having a different position in a value hierarchy. Thus we distinguish between a humanitarian value and an emotional sympathetic response. We deny that there are any circumstances, not entailing other values, that permit a man to act inhumanely; on the other hand, the number of circumstances where we permit a man normally called sympathetic to act unsympathetically has no known limits: he may have a headache, be preoccupied with other matters, dislike the person or situation, and so on.

We also distinguish between values and tastes, wishes, etc by treating values as if they were logical propositions. It is not possible to affirm both P and Not-P if P is a value judgement, whereas we see no contradiction if it is not. Thus, should a man assert that cruelty is wrong and corporal punishment right, we demand an explanation of the apparent inconsistency; yet a man who asserts that he both wants, and does not want, to go to the theatre is not required to explain his ambivalence, and probably could not. Feelings are not expected to follow the principles of logic.

There are other characteristics of value judgements that distinguish them from the phenomena with which they are sometimes identified. However, enough has been said to establish that men do make empirical distinctions and consequently that whatever it is the relativists are talking about, they are not referring to values as we know them.

But there is another reason for being dissatisfied with the relativist viewpoint: relativists appear to have ignored the function of norms. Certainly if norms have the nature attributed to them by relativists, they cannot have any particularly significant function for either the individual or society. Regarded as tastes or attitudes of individuals, some of them can conceivably serve private interests if other individuals can somehow be led to suppose they are something else; regarded as customs they can serve to maintain an in-group out-group division that in certain circumstances could be advantageous. But if this is all that norms can do, the extraordinary passions that have arisen when they are violated are very difficult to understand. The relativist's norms seem, in fact, of little importance.

Yet norms having characteristics which which we can observe empirically are essential to both individuals and societies, for they represent principles of choice, goals for which men strive. Without them, our choices would be determined by our biological drives and the particular conditions surrounding us. In such circumstances, the social order necessary for man's continuance as a species would be impossible, unless we were willing to regard foresight and identification of the individual with the species as biological drives. Furthermore, we would repeatedly find ourselves in the situation of Buridan's Ass, which was unable to act because there was no way of making a choice. What relativists overlook is that if norms are to function as principles of choice, they must both be limited in number and ordered into systems. Unordered and unrelated wishes or tastes can have no real function, or rather would be disfunctional, leading to conflicts both within the individual and between individuals that would be incompatible with the continuance of human life. What the advocate of natural law needs to study are the principles of choice and the order they must have if man is to continue on this earth. The choices men actually make—their habits, tastes, attitudes, customs and impulses—are not his concern.

'Relative' Natural Law

To serve their function of ordering the life of the individual and the community, norms must have the characteristics we ordinarily attribute to them, rather than those the relativists assign. Thus when we suppose that some norms do not simply represent the interests of the believer or the community, but are demanded by the nature of community life we are deluding ourselves; but the delusion is inescapable. We must act as if the norms had an authority that did not stem solely from the fact that we accept them. They must be regarded as more than goals we have chosen, obligations we have assumed, or limitations we have imposed: otherwise, they will not be observed with sufficient consistency or inculcated with sufficient conviction to serve their ordering function.

Such a view is quite compatible with relativism and brings us no nearer to anything resembling the traditional conception of natural law. It resembles what some tend to call 'relative natural law'. This is the view that all societies must make assumptions about the directions in which they move, and adhere to them. They could have made other assumptions—conceivably any that would be consistent with the continuance of human life in a community—but the ones that have been made are as good as any alternative.

Modified in this way, relativism can make a much more convincing case than does the mere equation of interests and norms. By recognizing the function of norms—and with it the necessary rational element—the modified theory can account for the recurrence in unrelated societies of similar patterns of norms, such as the family, property ownership, and the prohibition of in-group killing, without retreating from the fundamental relativist view that none of these are prescribed by the nature of things. They are prescribed only by the nature of certain widespread social orders and the nature of a functioning normative code. Nothing is prescribed by the nature of things: no 'is' can become an 'ought'.

Such a view, however, requires us to suppose that we have always deluded ourselves about norms and that we must continue to do so even after the relativists have opened our eyes to the true nature of norms, for if we do not, norms will not serve their function. If we admit that the relativist contention is true, norms become conveniences of the society which any member may at any time find it convenient to ignore. In other words, they will not function as norms if the function alone commends them. They have to be believed in, always; but if the belief is felt to be a matter of choice, this will not happen. The shift from the simple equation of wish and norm, in order to accommodate the social function of norms, makes their observance incomprehensible.

It may seem at first that no real problem has been raised, that the school of relative natural law is arguing for no more than the observance of custom; this has been generally felt to be binding and it is now reinforced by the argument that no other norms could be more binding. Now, it is true that when norms are challenged, men have repeatedly retreated to the logic-tight compartment of 'Well, that is what I believe. That is the way we do things here.' In consequence, it seems as if the ways of society are observed because they are the ways of society. But we must not assume that the answer necessarily represents the 'real' motive for observing the norm. It could not. There is nothing in a custom that compels its observance, unless it is felt to be something more than a custom. Custom as custom is not appealed to unless it is felt to represent divinely appointed ways, the wisdom of the past or something else distinguishing it from habitual ways of doing things, which have always been felt to be conveniences only and not something that we must impose on ourselves or others. Indeed, customs are distinguished from norms by the feeling that observance of the custom is a matter of choice for those who can think of another way of doing things. Observance of the norm, on the other hand, is requisite, a distinction that the man who falls back on custom as an explanation for a norm will himself make.

Who Shall Determine Natural Law and How?

The question of who shall determine natural law is directly

related to the question of whether men would recognize the validity of natural law if it could be shown to exist. That men do suppose that 'natural law' necessitates an obligation to observe it, may be seen from the fact that they justify the norms they follow on the ground that they are 'natural'. Perfecting one's nature or fulfilling natural tendencies can only be a requirement of natural law and not a justification of the concept—men do justify their norms by appealing to a supposed 'is' of their nature, even though they may never have heard of natural law. The reason would seem to lie in man's recognition that to serve the function of supplying directions and ordering human relations, norms must be of such a character that they can be self-imposed; the only ones that could be so imposed are those that are supposed to be in one's long-range interests. Here, the interests of the 'self' are viewed as having a future which must be taken into account in making choices, and the 'self' as having a nature that can be distorted and interfered with by society and the demands of custom.

Imposed by an external authority, norms come to be seen as restrictions on the self rather than methods of developing or fulfilling it, and hence become something to be evaded whenever possible. Thus they cease to serve their function for the individual and become techniques of maintaining social harmony. But the 'harmony' is a precarious one, which exists only when a coercive authority is present. It results in a conflict of interest between individual and community, community and state, that has been the principal source of disorder in human relations. It is true that this conflict can be reduced by the subtler kinds of coercion: for instance, the types of control which Plato advocated in *The Republic*. But such techniques, even if they were effective (and obviously they are not), merely shift the problem of alienation from the masses to the élite, so that society, instead of having to fear rebellion by the mob, is confronted with the 'treason of the clerks'. Those responsible for controlling the public remain unconvinced themselves about the 'rightness' of their behaviour, except as an expedient. But expediency, or submission to the demands of circumstances and immediate interests, can serve only the needs of the dependent or the subordinate. (The child knows the family will protect him, the shiftless alcoholic knows that the humanitarian principles held by others will not permit him to destroy himself utterly.) It cannot serve the needs of the 'Guardians' who, as humans, must also have norms that seem to be natural laws. No one can devote his life to inculcating and promoting what he does not believe in, unless he supposes there are 'natural' norms requiring it; in this case, they will be the norms he will inculcate, and he himself will exist only as a function, a non-self. He can deceive himself, of course, but if he is sufficiently deceived to suppose that the norms he is inculcating are natural laws when in fact they are not, he will provoke an attitude of inquiry and investigation that will lead to others being 'undeceived', so that his self-deception will work against the achievement of his aims. The problem posed by our need for values that are binding because of their nature cannot, then, be solved by self-deception or deception of any kind. What still remains is the problem posed by the need for norms that are not relative.

Who shall determine 'natural law', assuming it is a meaningful concept? If we leave it to the individual, we shall end up with what we have now—anarchic relativism—but without the one normative contribution of relativism—tolerance—that mitigates some of its worst social consequences. Natural law determined by the individual would be both relative and absolutist, differing from man to man but held by each with utter conviction and, presumably, utter intolerance for the 'errors' of others. But natural law determined by an organized body of investigators would fail to carry out its own obligation and thus would fail to serve its function.[2] If the law-makers escaped this difficulty by not only determining the law but establishing the sanctions for violating it, so that moral law

[2] An organized body, by its very nature, acquires a vested interest in its own functioning. No matter what an institution has been set up to accomplish, its first principle must be to maintain itself. If it supposes that it is the sole determinant of the 'good', it must be prepared to abandon that good, temporarily, if its existence is threatened by continuing to promote it. To act otherwise would be to deny its purpose. Most of us are aware of this 'law of the institution'. It lies at the root of our enduring suspicion of Church and State, which have always—not unnaturally—shown a readiness to accommodate their principles to circumstances. An organized body promoting natural law, then, would not be acceptable.

became a kind of positive law, the state would become a minutely regulated police state.

These two methods of determining natural law are not, of course, the only possibilities. Orderly investigation of the possibilities by trained observers need not imply state control. In liberal democracies both science and philosophy have remained reasonably free from outside interference. However, neither has been particularly helpful to natural law: their analyses of what we have believed to be natural laws have merely fostered our doubts; moreover, each discipline is at present committed to the view that there can be no such thing as natural law. Each ignores the fact that we must act as if our norms were natural laws. The moment a norm is felt to be a mere convention or ceases to bind us, it no longer serves as a long-range goal and a reliable method of making decisions in our 'real' interest. There is something wrong with an approach that tells us in effect that we do not have any long-range interests.

Philosophy has failed to be of any real service in the investigation of natural law because it has examined the question from the wrong angle, largely because of its Greek heritage. When the philosopher thinks of man's 'nature' he tends to think of it as the Greeks did, as something having an essential being or essence which would, if an 'ought' could come from an 'is', give rise to a single criterion of 'the good', which would serve as the ultimate standard for measuring particular 'goods' and thus enable us to decide which norms had precedence in any particular situation. It would certainly solve many problems if we could think of man's nature in this way, but we cannot. We no longer believe in essences. If the concept of man's nature is to be meaningful, it must do so as a composite of attributes which have no necessary order. From such a nature we cannot derive a single principle that will enable us to order our norms. Given the obvious fact that man as we know him is the product of his norms, it is useless to attempt to abstract the norms so as to discover the nature, and derive valid norms. We are looking at the problem in the wrong way. The problem is that we need norms having the characteristics of natural law, whereas the norms we have do not in fact have the necessary characteristics, or cannot be shown to possess them. The problem is *not* that we do not have norms. We do not necessarily need to find something new. What we need to do is to examine our doubts.

Man has always tried to cope with doubts about norms by silencing them—advocating better 'socialization', and more and more ingenious interpretations of the 'real' meaning of the norms. But such methods do not serve the purpose. It is possible to silence in particular men's doubts about, say, equality by giving it a non-historical interpretation.[3] But such dishonesty defeats itself, for if the interpretation is ingenious enough to override doubts, it becomes too detached from reality to serve any real function. Thus, for the thoughtful man of today the (alleged) norm 'equality' is an empty verbalism. It has been given so many interpretations that no one who questions its validity can act on it as a norm, so that it becomes devoid of content and remains a source of dissatisfaction.

Ingenious 'rationalizations' can serve no useful purpose. What is needed is strict honesty in setting out the logical consequences of acceptance of the norm as something capable of prescribing a type of behaviour. If it is given such an interpretation that nothing follows, it ceases to be a norm. This appears to have happened with norms that formerly had a clear-cut meaning, such as 'honour'. In feudal times, the latter prescribed the kind of behaviour that Hotspur believed in, but which became inappropriate to the Renaissance society and then was given so many interpretations that it could no longer act as a norm and became a mere word of approval. The same thing seems to be happening with 'equality'. It does not help to argue that equality 'really' means equality before the law, equality of opportunity etc. We only add to our difficulties with the egalitarian norm by giving it specialized and non-historical interpretations. Our problem, namely our doubt, arises from the fact that once upon a time we did suppose that men were

---

[3] Historically, modern egalitarianism has unmistakable links with puritanism. The puritan, with his doctrine that each man must seek his own salvation, was logically compelled to believe that all men were created equal: variations in innate ability to be 'good' would make free competition for salvation a manifest injustice.

equal—or could be—and structured the norm into our society; as a result, we now have a number of practices, such as majority rule, universal franchise and public education, which cannot be defended in terms of the norm because the norm itself is not defensible.

Some of the practices themselves have important normative consequences. There is, for instance, an obvious relationship between the majority rule norm and relativism, anti-rationalism and aberrations of individualism which are characteristic of our society. When we have doubts about norms, this is the kind of problem we have in mind and ingenious re-interpretations are of no assistance. Our difficulty is not that we do not have norms in which we believe; we do, and must, have them. It is that we are not sure what all their consequences are, and that misguided persons have been trying to disguise the problem. Until we can set out—without apology, rationalization and re-interpretation of the norms we hold—the types of behaviour demanded and the intricate relationships between them, we cannot even begin to discuss natural law. The only evidence we have about the nature of man is his norms. Amazingly enough, no one has yet attempted to record and relate them. Even when we perform this very necessary task, we shall still be not a whit closer to solving the 'is-ought' problem, but we shall at least have a surer basis for making rational decisions about the directions in which we wish to go.

Positive and Natural Law and Ideology

In a society whose elective system requires a relativist outlook to justify it, whose pluralist structure finds the seeming tolerance of relativism useful in preserving harmony, and whose philosophers have provided a logical defence for relativism, there would seem to be no place for natural law. Yet some kind of law applicable to all members of the society, some statement about what is permissible and what is not, the goals to be pursued and so forth, is clearly necessary to social order. Even the most extreme relativists have agreed on that. But in their eyes the supposition that the law of the land can be, or should be, measured against some other law of 'reason', 'conscience' or 'nature' is an illusion fostered by conditions that no longer prevail. In past times, men have used concepts of natural law to overthrow systems of government that sought to impose norms incompatible with the actual norms of society, or to overthrow governments insufficiently responsive to the requirements of the society's norms. Present-day governments, however, have learnt the lesson of relativism, which is in part the lesson of sovereignty: a government derives its power from being recognized as the source of order, which ensures continuity of the society's norms. If it takes sides in normative disputes (except ideological disputes affecting its authority), it abandons its function as a government. Should it seek to impose new norms that conflict with those of the society, it would misunderstand its own position and the nature of norms. The normative problem facing governments today is to teach the people that they deny their government the authority to uphold the norms they believe in, if they assume that there is a non-arbitrary standard by which to judge the government's performance.

This is a plausible view which allows room for both natural law—or rather the belief in it—and positive law, and which ensures that no major conflicts between the two will arise. The plausibility of such relativism rests on its apparent ability to reconcile the positive and negative aspects of norms through the medium of a particular type of government. In effect, it argues that if a government allows its policy to be determined by the norms of the group it governs—the ideology which becomes for it a kind of natural law—it will be supplied with the goals necessary for action and will be able to restrict the goals of its citizens to ensure social order. The nature of the ideology appears to be of no importance, provided it enables the system to exist; nor does it seem to matter in the least what the positive law is, provided it is compatible with the ideology. But these aspects do matter. Such relativism makes 'reason', 'conscience' and 'nature', when applied to norms, simply inaccurate terms for what the relativist really regards as 'taste', 'desire' and 'custom'. The relativist asserts that had those who had put forward these standards of natural law been raised in a different environment, their 'reason' and 'conscience' would have led in quite different directions. To suppose that they would not have done so is an aberration induced by a particular environment; consequently, it is in the interest of both the state and the community to try to remove it. Yet it is precisely the claims of 'reason' and 'conscience' that lie behind democratic individualism, which is utterly indefensible if interpreted as a demand to pursue self-interest. Furthermore, to deny that norms contain a rational element converts the problem of 'authority' from one of 'obligation' to one of coercion. Under relativism, men are no longer thought to obey because they recognize merit in the system—that would be an illusion—but because through education, habit, tradition and the open and concealed influence exerted by the state they are coerced from birth into accepting the system. Consequently, all functioning norms in the society (as distinct from verbal platitudes inherited from the past) must partake of the nature of positive law. Even the ideology must somehow be enforced.

There are other obstacles when one attempts to make an ideology serve all the functions of natural law or supposed natural law. The democratic ideology, at least, was not designed for that purpose. Its two basic norms—individualism and egalitarianism—and the 'natural rights' related to them were directed toward supplying the social conditions necessary to develop the 'self' which, guided by 'reason' and 'conscience', would be capable of recognizing what natural law commanded. As such they were presumably felt to be a part of natural law, but not the whole of it. (It is true, of course, that a utilitarian ethic can be extracted from simple individualism and egalitarianism, as shown by the history of philosophy from Hobbes onwards; but apart from the philosophic weakness in utilitarianism, it cannot yield all the norms current in a society.)

There are also difficulties in deciding just what the ideology requires. Are we to reason (as many right-wing conservatives still do) that since all men are equal, differences in achievement and in its concomitant material reward are a just reflection of the individual will, and hence that a sense of responsibility for the poor is misguided sympathy for the feckless and that welfare schemes defeat their purpose? Or should we adopt a left-wing radical view that a disproportionate achievement represents some kind of cheating and exploitation? We could also choose the current left-of-centre view that there are the 'privileged' and the 'underprivileged' and spend our time thinking of schemes to create what is called 'equality of opportunity'. The ideology does not provide an answer for so simple a question, but it does provide scope for serious conflicts of opinion, for the interpretation we make in one area must be carried over into others.

To derive a multiplicity of norms from a basic set of one or two requires such close reasoning that adherents of the various possibilities are driven to form camps. Thus the man who interprets achievement in terms of will commits himself to the view that crime is also a matter of will, to which the environment is irrelevant, so that in his opinion punishment is the answer to crime and strict equality (or uniformity) of treatment the mark of justice. For the 'environmentalist', however, equality before the law is a monstrous injustice and punishment a medieval aberration. The entire field of the social sciences is riddled with these camps, all of them certain that they are pursuing pure science when they are, in fact, taking up normative positions derived from democratic ideology and adapted to their personal tastes.

Since relativism and egalitarianism are closely related and egalitarianism is a widely accepted norm today, it is decidedly inconvenient to find that ideology will not serve the function of natural law. It is quite clear that positive law alone is not sufficient. Positive law detached from any form of natural law or (to use behaviouralist jargon) 'legitimation device', is enforceable only if it is in the self-interest of the citizen to observe it either by adapting it to his self-interest (which would make it no law at all) or by applying appropriate sanctions. Since the enforcement of even one generally unpopular law would strain the state's enforcement resources, the need to treat all citizens, in regard to all laws, as criminals at heart could not be permanently met; moreover, if all the norms of a society partook of the nature of positive law, the state would lack the social organization needed to enforce the law.

Relativists try to overcome this difficulty by treating part of the law—the ideology, constitution or norm of norms—as both a kind of positive law and a kind of natural law: in other words, if one can accept the constitution as legitimate, then any laws passed in accordance with the requirements of that constitution must be regarded as legitimate. But this view only proves that even convinced relativists acknowledge some natural law assumptions to be necessary.[4]

[4] Several other problems arise if natural law is excluded and all functioning norms are derived from positive law alone. Positive law—despite its name—is basically negative. We have not developed, nor are we likely to develop, workable techniques of commanding anything but the most specific tasks. We do not know how to order someone to be industrious, tolerant or democratic because we cannot set forth the specifications, or imagine what sanctions could be applied if people failed to fulfill them. Positive law is more effective when prohibiting specific types of behaviour, but even here it must rely on a general willingness to obey the spirit of the law rather than the letter, for even the most minutely detailed and carefully worded laws can be evaded by the wily.

Chapter VI

From Natural Law to Public Philosophy

The practice which democratic governments have of continually legislating prevents anyone from being convinced that an appeal to positive law is an appeal to fundamental principles. Yet there are overriding principles of legislation and these do incorporate natural law principles. Consequently, democratic societies have felt free to legislate on matters that would seem to lie outside their jurisdiction, such as drugs, alcohol and sexual behaviour.[1]

'Applied' Natural Law in Democratic Societies

One cannot be sure which factors are decisive when laws are changed, and it is particularly hard to detect evidence of an attempt to apply conceptions of natural law. This is because the norms of natural law are primarily statements about goals which seldom can be directly 'commanded' by positive law. Thus even if everyone were to agree that natural law demands pride of craftmanship and working to the best of one's ability, it is not possible for positive law to demand this—a fact

---

[1] It must be admitted that legislation on such matters has been both defended and attacked on purely relativist grounds: some have argued that it is justifiable only if it represents 'majority' public opinion, while others have held that it is never justifiable even if it does, since the issues are purely private. Both opinions represent different schools of relativism. It would seem, however, that neither school can adequately explain why such legislation continues in force, or why the changes being made in it are taking the form they do.

discovered by communists and bureaucrats of all persuasions. Positive law intended to reflect a natural law norm of craftmanship would have to be directed towards creating the conditions believed to promote the norm, and the influence of the norm would not be directly discernible in the legislation. The actual norms being applied in legislation can usually be discovered only by listening to the justifications given, and by noting the absence or elimination of certain types of legislation which might be expected if natural law norms were not being considered.

Clearly, a principle is needed to allow us to detect the operation of natural law norms or assumed natural law norms in legislation. For example, whenever the movement is towards consistency in principle and orderly legislation, there is a strong presumption that the strict relativism of classical democratic theory has been abandoned. Unfortunately, the principle of consistency cannot be used to detect all applications of supposed natural law, because natural law demands the pursuit of goals which cannot be directly expressed in positive law. It is partly for this reason that it is not easy to decide what principles lie behind modern legislation on the use of alcohol and drugs. What is the basis for a democratic society's right to legislate on these matters? To call it simply a carryover of Puritan legislation cannot explain this. Rather we might guess from the general tendency of much legislation in recent years—compulsory seat-belts for motorists and crash helmets for motor cyclists, compulsory pension plans, compulsory health insurance and so forth—that the state is attempting to impose prudence on those who are irresponsible, or lack foresight and common sense. The state is reluctant to admit that what is objectionable about drugs is the attitude to life, the uninhibited hedonism, implied by the deliberate use of sense excitants. But it cannot tolerate such hedonism, which expresses an attitude possible only for those who can depend on the work and sense of responsibility of others. This attitude places the democratic state in an awkward position. Positive law in this instance can at best be no more than a stop-gap measure. Laws have no effect on causes and, if enforced in such cases, evoke criticism of the government not only on the ground of democratic principles but also on that of hedonism itself. It may not be enough for the state, then, to attempt the present 'gingerly' application of principles of natural law. It will probably have to become more frank or more 'Hegelian'.

What is inherent in the nature of government is a demand for reason. Unlike the private citizen, government cannot leave its motives undisclosed. To safeguard its own existence, it must weigh the probable consequences of a policy before initiating it; hence, even though relative principles have entered its calculations, it must go a step beyond relativism towards natural law. Not desire or custom, but 'reasonableness in action'—which d'Entrèves sees as the essence of natural law [2]—must characterize the action of a viable government. Granted that there are natural law norms and that it is best to live in accordance with them, any government not based on force (which exempts it from the requirement of being rational) and not so premised on relativist norms that it can never call them into question, will move towards the discovery and application of natural law.

The process by which it does so is quite unlike that which natural law postulates as necessary: it does not go back to, and reason from, first principles, but works within the framework of existing norms. Advocates of natural law feel that this method is dangerous, believing that the reasonableness desired can be most easily obtained by abandoning awkward norms. Such simplification is indeed characteristic of most private citizens, who seem to imagine that if they reduce normative issues to some simple requirement, such as being law-abiding or going to church, they have done all that good men should. A government, however, cannot over-simplify in this way, for the norms with which it must work remain present in society whether it chooses to observe them or not.

[2] See A P d'Entrèves, *Natural Law* (Hutchinson, London, 1970), p 78. The use of 'reasonableness' rather than 'reason' is in itself a valuable contribution to the discussion of natural law, for unlike the latter term with its multiple meanings, 'reasonableness' conveys simply the idea of moderation and of being open to discussion. It makes no appeal to an ultimate standard which sets for all time the exact nature of the norm, so that d'Entrèves escapes the common charge that natural law advocates are seeking to establish absolutes to which all must conform even if they are unable to recognize them for what they are said to be.

One of the chief obstacles to the application of natural law principles in a democratic society is the presence of a norm which violates a fundamental requirement of natural law: equality is denied as a fact of human nature but accepted as a norm. The problem is the presence in a society of norms which are both recognized as relative and insisted upon as constituent elements, fundamental principles which are not open to question. When rational analysis is blocked in this way, there is no possibility of society ever developing or observing natural law norms, true 'reasonableness in action'. In small ways supposed natural law norms will be incorporated in legislation; but there will be no guarantee they will remain, or that any attempt will be made to ascertain whether they are indeed natural law norms. Unless reason is free to explore the assumptions also, and these are of special importance, we must regard the society as essentially coercive and therefore incompatible with the premises of natural law. Thus it is the democratic assumptions about equality (and individualism) that we must be free to criticize. The freedom to discuss all other principles—to be relativists—is not freedom enough.

Obligation and Two Sets of Societal Norms

The term 'natural law' has been opposed on the ground that its use carries with it so many outmoded and irrelevant traditions that it beclouds the very issue it should clarify: that in any society there are two sets of norms. One of these is the positive law, which has recognized methods for deriving and enforcing it; the other is the set of norms—some of whose elements may be peculiar to only a small number of individuals—which has no clear source and no established method of enforcement. For convenience, I shall refer to the second set of norms as 'natural law', even though I recognize that some of its elements may not be part of natural law as it is usually conceived. This seemingly high-handed procedure is possible here because only the interrelationship between the two sets of norms will be discussed. The validity of the content of neither set is at issue.

The jurist, even while recognizing that the best defence of positive law is a supposed basis in natural law, has always wished to make a clear distinction between them, in order the better to apply the rules of positive law. Otherwise, if there are vague rules within the community which may override his own, he has no clear way of determining what the law is, although he is compelled by the nature of his office to do so. The temptation for the jurist, then, is to assert that for him there can be only one law, the positive law, and that if others feel that a further set of valid laws exists, they can incorporate it into the set of positive laws. The difficulty is that the nature of the second set of norms, whether they are natural law norms or not, does not allow the positive law to remain independent.

In ethical problems raised by the question of natural law one cannot avoid the issue of responsibility. (The former are all problems of choice, and the question of whether and to what extent freedom of choice was present in violations immediately arises.) In theory, positive law can disregard responsibility and deal exclusively with crime and punishment; the judge in this instance is no more than one who sifts the evidence for and against the arraigned, and applies sanctions, if necessary, after all the evidence has been given. This, in fact, is what the concept of equality before the law implies: nothing is relevant except the existence of an alleged violation and the evidence for and against the person charged with the deed. 'Guilty' means 'did it'. Such a view simplifies the jurist's problem of applying the law, but increases the difficulty of enforcing it. (To disregard the relevance of free choice by ignoring responsibility entails disregarding the concept of obligation which is also present in questions of free choice.) The positive law would have to become purely coercive.

The jurist can partially escape this difficulty by incorporating some of the natural law criteria for establishing responsibility: for example, by establishing a legal age of responsibility and rules for deciding soundness of mind. But it is impossible to incorporate into any one law or set of laws all the possibilities required by natural law considerations.[3] For the law to give full

---

[3] This is because when establishing responsibility, the free choice we talk about requires us to consider not only whether the accused was capable of

consideration to ethical questions, it would have to include a statement about every possible interaction with every other possible norm under all conceivable conditions. We circumvent the problem by having the judge and jury sift the evidence not only for and against the existence of a factual violation by the arraigned, but also for and against his moral responsibility. The jurist has to accept the concept of responsibility in order to retain that of obligation.

Since the obligation to obey the positive law comes from its overlapping with natural law—its enforcement of an order that is already accepted as obligatory by most of the community—any serious disparity between the two orders reduces the sense of obligation. Because the order of importance in natural law cannot be disregarded, positive law can never exist in isolation: as a mere enumeration of norms, and penalties for violating them. Superimposed on it is an order of importance derived from the natural law system. But there are limits to any possible order of importance; positive law is basically coercive; and such order as it has, is becoming less and less marked as the possible sanctions are reduced. At one time positive law had a fairly complex order of preference which largely reflected society's views of the gravity of various crimes and the corresponding degrees of responsibility—degrees of pain could be inflicted that reflected varying degrees of social disapproval. This has been eliminated by the rise of the humanitarian value which will not tolerate cruel punishment; the coerciveness of the system of positive law has lost much of its logic; and the view has been reinforced that it should perhaps not be coercive at all and should become more like natural law.

Ethical Considerations in Positive Law

The concept of sovereignty puts the jurist in an ambiguous position as regards the relationship of justice to ethics. On the

---

making the kind of choice a normal person makes, but also whether the latter choice would have been the right one. In other words, we raise the question whether in violating one norm, the accused was obeying another and equally valid one.

one hand, the judge—as an agent of the sovereign—must view the law as a set of procedural rules which he must follow if he is to fulfill the conditions of his office. If he views the law in the same way as the sovereign presumably regards it—as rules of social order which must be enforced if the sovereign is to fulfill his function and thus remain sovereign—the judge oversteps the limits of his delegated power and usurps part of the sovereign's function. The moment the judge attempts to follow the intent rather than the letter of the law, he himself becomes in part a law-giver whose private judgement of what is necessary to social order acquires at least as much importance as that of the sovereign. In practice it acquires more importance: it is the interpretation and application of the law that constitutes the law of the land, rather than the sovereign decree on which it is theoretically based. Such a situation, however, is not satisfactory even to the judge—even though he may enjoy the power it entails—for his very authority depends upon his position in a power structure of which he is a subordinate member. As a jurist, he is in no position to take the comprehensive view of society as a whole which the sovereign takes before deciding an issue.

On the other hand, the judge cannot limit himself to the letter of the law. As a functionary in an operating system of sovereignty he has to accept the premise that to maintain order, the sovereign must be prepared to right all wrongs: private revenge is not tolerable. For the judge, this means that for every wrong there must be a remedy—one of the primary maxims of equity. But to ensure this through the medium of a set of positive laws is beyond the power of positive law, which is utterly incapable of foreseeing all possible combinations of circumstances and setting down regulations minute enough to supply the judge with rules of procedure enabling him to remain a pure functionary. Indeed, the principal argument against the juristic conception of sovereignty, which makes the law or its supreme norm the sovereign, lies in just this consideration: only if the law is regarded as a functionless set of rules is it complete. As part of a functioning system which maintains order, it is always incomplete. Someone or something else must complete it, namely the political sovereign; but he, by the nature of the system, cannot himself be the judge.[4]

The requirements of sovereignty which cannot tolerate conflicting authorities, or permit an independent authority to exist within its system, have eliminated 'conscience' from the law and with it, one feels, any possibility of ethical considerations playing a role in the legal system. Though there is a common law maxim *ubi jus, ibi remedium* paralleling the equity maxim 'Equity will not suffer a wrong to be without a remedy',[5] it is not possible for the judge to attempt to implement it. The principle of sovereignty requires him to be bound by law, not conscience. Our society tries to surmount this difficulty by having a continuous system of law-making, but from the point of view of ethics, the method is unsatisfactory. In the first place, the laws it passes must be general, directed against circumstances which give rise to what seems to be injustice, whereas ethics requires an analysis of particular circumstances before judgement is passed. To suppose that positive law by itself can create justice is like supposing that the desire to be good is the same as being good: that if everyone is compelled to be just, justice will prevail. But, of course, an unwillingness to be just is not an issue in ethics, which deals primarily with what is the good and when one is good, rather than with the question of whether one is willing to be good and how to attain it. The assumption of 'good will' is necessary to any discussion of ethical problems. The law, however, must assume ill will if it is to operate. It cannot punish mere mistakes of judgement, though it must insist on a redress of private wrong if it is to fulfill its function of maintaining order: that is, if it is to be a system whereby the vagaries of private revenge are replaced by institutional forms which in some way compensate for the wrong done. For this to happen there must be an agreement about what have been the good under the particular circumstances in which an injury has supposedly been inflicted. The law cannot determine this: only the judge can. But if he attempts to do so, he creates a 'precedent': a particular law deriving from circumstances that for him are binding,

[4] This is made clear by the history of equity. See G W Keeton, *An Introduction to Equity* (Pitman, London, 1965), pp 2 ff.
[5] *Ibid*, p 87.

presumably because they accord with his conception of justice, and that are made binding upon other judges who may not have the same hierarchy of values as the judge who set the precedent. In the absence of a clear hierarchy of values, then, the judge is forced willy-nilly to fall back on his private hierarchy of norms and require their acceptance by the parties to the dispute—even though this is contrary to the principles of sovereignty, which require the order to come from the top of the hierarchy, not from functionaries lower down, where the order is applied. Indeed, the moment disputants feel that the decision is the product of a private interpretation, the decision is no longer acceptable. The only really binding decision for them is one from which there can be no appeal whatever. It is an unmistakable contradiction to assert that X is both a subordinate decision-maker and an ultimate decision-maker. Under the system now prevailing, disputes about nature of the just decision are inevitable and the disagreement cannot be resolved by asserting that at some future date the true sovereign—parliament, perhaps—will right future wrongs.

Further, a law that seeks to remedy an injustice under our system is always *ex post facto*: it can perhaps prevent a recurrence of injustice, but it can do little about injustices that have already been committed. Nor will a law which deletes an act from the list of crimes necessarily open prison doors for those undergoing punishment for having committed it. This is one of the difficulties induced by our attitude to *ex post facto* laws. Because we feel it unjust to make an act punishable after it has been committed, we find it difficult to apply a law abolishing an act as punishable to those already being punished for having committed it. Both are *ex post facto* changes. We cannot leave the matter to the jurists: they act only when compelled to. And we cannot expect the sovereign to remedy past errors, because this would raise doubts about his competency. It is a perplexing problem which arises often in ethics, but it causes no practical difficulties, since an ethical judgement need not be final. The law, on the other hand, must make a final decision.

The Problem of Democracy and 'Natural Law'

Historically, modern democracy in the Western world and natural law have been closely associated. Unlike all other political orders, democracy has not had to propagate itself through force of arms or organized subversion or, until recently, to rely on custom for its continuance. Men have clearly believed that the particular political order it prescribes in some way reflects a natural order deriving from the nature of man, or prescribed by the nature of things. The 'sacrosanct' democratic constitutions seem to have acquired their authority from a supposed reflection of a higher order rather than from respect for tradition or the law, for they have been 'inviolable' from the moment of their enactment in a way that other laws have not. Against the fact of state power, the democratic value order has set the rights of the individual—based on an appeal to an order superior to that of the state.

Yet democracy as it is commonly conceived, and natural law as it is traditionally understood, are incompatible. Democracy regarded as a social order expressing the wishes of the people or the rule of the majority, and natural law interpreted as a set of universal norms, can hardly co-exist, for the first is an expression of relativism and the second of 'absolutism'.

Even if relativism could be shown to be philosophically unsound, it would remain the basic ethical position of any society which assumes that the rule of the majority must decide social issues. If we are to hold to the majority rule, we must abandon the view that a good can exist apart from what society says. 'The good' and the wishes of the people become identified with one another.

This attitude has been resisted vigorously by the Church, which would like to function (as it did at the inception of democracy) as a moral arbiter. But those religions which have held to the view that there is a higher order have inevitably found themselves in the curious position of being attacked from the moral standpoint—on the ground that their standards are artificial and unrealistic. It is how people actually behave, rather than statements about how they should behave, that sets the standards which most people are ready to accept.

If human beings were molecules, we could be satisfied with the present situation. Subject to the effects of a universal law of causation, we would cease worrying about what was going to happen next. But the apparent—perhaps illusory—human capacity to take action not only in accordance with drives which are part of the causal chain, but also with sets of values—which we invent and from which we make a selection, on grounds other than the fact that we invented them—seems to have introduced a new element which enables us to choose, or not choose, to act. Without a set of values, we cannot act socially at all. Biological drives and their interrelation with the physical environment are irrelevant socially, except as values or in so far as the forms they take make them relevant. Drives are private needs which can be satisfied only socially and under social restraints. To ensure their satisfaction social forms are necessary, as well as other values over and above those deriving from our biological being.

Who is to order those values? The inherent democratic predilection for relativism is the basic difficulty: relativists ignore the problem of order, identifying norms and tastes. It is true that members of our society have been, as best they can, working out systems of values for themselves on the assumption that biological drives are the source of some valid norms. But 'drives' provide no real explanation of human behaviour. The issue they raise is not that of 'I must' but 'What will I do?' Even if members of our society were right as to their own assumptions regarding the control of their behaviour and were able to provide a fully working guide, the problem would remain unsolved because the government—which is supposed to integrate our activity—has no equivalent guide. Without ceasing to be a government it cannot assume that the values of individual citizens must also be its own. (Thus the concept of 'responsible' government brings us remarkably close to certain difficulties in the Hobbesian concept of sovereignty.) Nor can it simply 'adjust' to circumstances or the facts. 'Oughts' or goals cannot arise from statements of what 'is', or from facts. The existence of an unbridged river is not proof that a bridge should be built.

The democratic predicament is that whereas, on the one hand, we have evolved a political system which requires some value order other than relativism—which is suited only to the original democratic assumption that we do not really need a government—on the other hand, the relativism which is inextricably linked with democratic forms precludes any other kind of value order.

Public Philosophy

Although—as is shown by public opinion surveys—people generally profess traditional democratic norms, few try to live up to them. Responsibility for the preservation of norms has been shifted to the government on the grounds that it is the 'duty' of democratically elected governments to operate within the framework of norms. But under present conditions it is not possible for the government to fulfill this role, just as it is not possible for the few 'natural law' norms of democracy to constitute and preserve a full code of 'civility'. Yet principles with the characteristics of 'natural law' norms are needed because we are rational beings capable of seeing that norms are necessary to action. Since the democratic system of government can no longer simply look to the governed for its 'will', the sovereign state, in order to govern, must develop its own principles of action and choice: a normless government has no will; a government which has no will cannot govern. What is needed is a shift in attitude from the private standard of taste and 'opinion' in the modern sense to the public standard of reason.

Public philosophy—Walter Lippmann's new term for natural law—helps eliminate some of the objections to the concept of 'natural law' and in an age of relativism makes it acceptable without fundamentally altering its nature. 'The public philosophy is known as *natural law*', says Lippmann, adding sadly in parenthesis that it is 'a name which, alas, causes great semantic confusion.'[6] Everything Lippmann says about public philosophy can be found in debates on natural law; the new term, however, focusses on certain central issues obscured by the earlier view of natural law as a concept for theologians. This view has affected modern democracy, which derives its fundamental constitutional assumptions from theological conceptions of man. Hobbes' conception of natural law did not receive its due attention because it was so thoroughly secular; and the concept of sovereignty he derived from 'natural law' seemed too impious for the protestant-democratic orders which were evolving during his time. Democratic states are now secularized; and if the fundamental assumptions of democratic societies are not to become empty formulas, we need to re-examine natural law. By getting rid of some semantic confusion, Lippmann's new term will enable us to move in that direction.

Of crucial importance is the theory of sovereignty. It is needed to account for the facts concerning our normative behaviour—our acceptance of both our own private set of norms and those expressed by the positive law of the state. 'Public philosophy' in political theory is the term applied here to the normative set—differing by the logic of sovereignty from the set held by any member of the public—which 'motivates' the state in the same way that the individual's norms motivate him. It is unfortunate that one should find it necessary to assert the need for public philosophy at a time when philosophy finds itself arrested in its normative analysis by relativism. It is not certain that political theory can analyse the content of 'public philosophy' without retreating from the logic of sovereignty which has given rise to the concept. The temptation for the political scientist is to analyse the policy of governments and call the generalizations that result 'public philosophy', just as the practice of relativists is to refer to generalized descriptions of human behaviour as 'the norms' of the individual. To the theorist, such an attempt to arrive at the norms of public

---

[6] Walter Lippmann, *Essays in the Public Philosophy* (Little, Brown and Company, Boston, 1955), p 101.

philosophy violates the line of thought which has led to the concept. Yet how is he to proceed when philosophy itself neither recognizes the need to relate the norms of positive law to the norms of the individual, nor realizes that the theory of sovereignty is necessary to the description of normative behaviour as we know it?

Chapter VII

The Consequences of Relativism and Behaviouralism

Despite general exposure to various types of absolutist ethics, one of the most striking characteristics of our society is pervasive relativism. It extends to several areas and is of many types: cultural, ethical, scientific, sociological, psychological, epistemological, etc. However, it is not the present purpose to focus on definitions of the various kinds of relativism, for this would prevent our grasping modern relativism in a total sense—seeing it as part of an all-inclusive system established by our society in which factors promoting relativism[1] form interlocking patterns. Once one makes an assumption or accepts a single value statement made by our society one is bound to accept the whole pattern and with it, relativism. The purpose of this study is to reveal this all-pervasive attitude and its relation to socio-political theorizing. This, of course, does not mean that the question of defining relativism is being avoided.

---

[1] Abraham Edel (*Ethical Judgment*, The Free Press, Glencoe, Illinois, 1955) speaks of several 'threads' [in the fabric of relativism]: (1) morality is a human product (2) everything changes (3) individual egoism (4) the struggle for power (5) mechanistic psychological and educational theory (6) cultural relativity (7) influence of the linguistic school of philosophy. (Incidentally, the metaphor 'threads that run through ... fabric' does not make it clear whether Edel is referring to factors within a society which promote relativism, or whether he is speaking of what is involved in it and serves to indicate its presence.) Edel's views, although interesting, lack a logical pattern. This reflects in part the relativistic view that culture and its elements do not form anything approaching a logical order. Otherwise grave doubts could be cast on relativism, which derives its chief strength from the seeming arbitrariness of cultural phenomena!

The Essence of Modern Relativism

The view that what is regarded as right action or the goodness of an objective may vary from place to place, time to time and even from individual to individual, has had a long history. It was held by the Sophists and it is held today. Modern relativism, however, differs quite markedly from earlier types. In the case of Thrasymachus's argument, for instance, it is clear that his concern is with the problem of why norms appear to be absolute; the 'appearance' of absolutism is the real problem and relativism is merely an assumption, a device for solving that problem. Modern relativism, on the other hand, is never just an assumption.

Western civilization has such a long tradition of Christian absolutist ethics that until the modern era relativism was accepted with considerable reluctance. Only since man began to see himself as limited to this world and (as national boundaries became fixed in many ways) restricted to the society in which he lived, and only since appropriate ideologies were developed, has it been possible to accept relativism with any enthusiasm. It has now become one of the main supports for political systems which incorporate egalitarianism as a norm: men who are convinced that an individual makes himself and shapes society according to his personality are emotionally committed to relativism.

This is not tantamount to asserting that relativism is little more than a normative attitude encouraged by most modern political systems. To say this would be to play Thrasymachus's game. Nor, in singling out the factors which helped to promote relativism, should one exaggerate the role of scepticism—often regarded as a relativistic attitude masquerading as a philosophy. On the contrary, scepticism is an element in a norm-directed, rather than relativistic, attitude.

By their nature, norms make universal assertions which—when applied to a particular situation—result in dilemmas and moral doubts characteristic of ethical discussion and moral behaviour. Men who feel sure of their norms invariably prove to be relativists relying on intuition, authority, or custom. All others—theologians, philosophers, the judiciary and individuals—who have striven throughout history to believe in absolute norms, have been compelled to question, analyse and 're-order' their norms. It is not possible to be moral—or be considered moral—without being sceptical about one's beliefs concerning past action. Scepticism is not to be confused with relativism, which denies the possibility of being sceptical about norms in any meaningful way.

The most significant single factor influencing the growth of relativism has been the impact on the study of norms of scientific method (which of course professes to incorporate scepticism). It may be argued that a method which eliminated teleological explanations is not well suited to the analysis of norms, which are essentially teleological—statements about ends and purposes, rather than descriptions of conditions. But scientific method claims to have universal application and its great success in analysing and interpreting physical phenomena has helped to maintain a persistent faith in the method itself, despite the fact that it has not produced a single general law of human behaviour to parallel the laws of physics. It is felt that the norms of a society must be as open to investigation by scientific method as any other process. People use 'oughts'; they also say that their 'oughts' impose an obligation to observe them. Is this true? Psychologists, anthropologists, political scientists and philosophers are all faced with this question. Although their particular approaches differ slightly, all reach the same conclusion: the 'oughts' cannot have the nature attributed to them by those who state them. The precise nature of these 'oughts' is uncertain: some may represent the goals of individuals or society; some may be inspired by social customs or self-interest; some are logical deductions from other 'oughts'. But the science-inspired conclusion is clear; it does not matter what they are so long as it can be shown that they are never absolute.

It is not only the absoluteness of norms that is questioned by relativists. Nearly all of the latter also deny the rational element in norms. For them, there is no point in analysing the consequences of normative patterns and ideologies. (They are equally indifferent to the consequences of the very outlook they adopt; relativism has become such an all-pervading factor in our society that even when it is not consciously accepted, it emerges in an implicit, ideological form.) From the relativist standpoint, man himself is not rational, so that normative analyses are irrelevant except to those who engage in them.

What happens to political philosophy when scientific method assumes a dominant rôle? If one's attitude to political philosophy is marked by strong empirical leanings, norms are reduced to abstractions and generalizations which bear only a remote relationship to human behaviour. When norms in the usual sense are discarded, political philosophy becomes an illusion.

Relativism and the Springs of Action: Norms as Tools of Analysis

Relativism has created a special problem for the student of human behaviour. At one time the tools of social analysis, norms, were regarded as being in the hands of all educated men. Norms were of a threefold nature: they appeared as descriptions of behaviour, explanations of why the behaviour had occurred, and judgements concerning the wisdom of that behaviour. Taking the first of these, the premise was that human behaviour was purposeful, in contrast to everything else in the universe, which was only caused. By examining behaviour and taking account of the circumstances, one could conjecture which norms had determined it; finally, from the consequences, one could decide whether it had been wise or not.

This approach made the whole of history available as evidence for the development of theories designed to show which would be the wisest course to follow. Men were not supposed to have always acted from similar motives or to have the same 'nature'. But it was assumed that all behaviour could be placed in normative categories which would explain it in such a way that men in later times would be able to understand it.

The tri-fold nature of norms, however, has worked against them in an age dominated by science. A description which is also a judgement has been considered a dangerous tool by scientists, who demand the elimination of normative judgements from the recording of 'facts'. The concept of purposeful action has also conflicted with the anti-teleological direction of science. The sharp division between human behaviour and the rest of creation required by the norm-directed attitude has seemed more an inheritance from theology than a justifiable scientific assumption. Consequently, norms in the traditional sense have been discarded as tools of analysis. Unfortunately for relativism, no substitute has been found, for relativism cannot supply one without losing its identity.

The social scientist is undoubtedly justified in being suspicious of the traditional normative categories: they are too vague and general, they overlap, and they are incomplete. But an ethically neutral equivalent which would supply something more than a description of unique phenomena seems impossible. Some principle of classification is necessary to obtain useful results, ie, results suited to a purpose. The moment we have a purpose, we adopt the basic normative view of human behaviour; once we require that the categories in our classification be explanations as well as descriptions, we find ourselves dealing with concepts which have the character of traditional norms. One can hardly escape the conclusion that relativists who wish to be 'true' scientists must stop being strict relativists. For norms are necessary tools of social analysis. Unless they are regarded as the springs of action, the real explanations must lie elsewhere, because of the very nature of the relativist interpretation of norms.

But what are the springs of action, and what method of classifying human behaviour is possible, when norms are discarded?[2] Analysts of social behaviour are repeatedly com-

---

[2] The rejection of norms as tools of analysis has also required each discipline in the social sciences to develop its own system of analytical categories. The possibility of finding a genuine interdisciplinary approach has vanished together with the norms. However, some of the categories which have developed—frustration, inferiority complex, sadism—acquire normative overtones as they become generally available concepts. It seems likely that the normative element was present from the beginning, that in fact it formed the selective principle which enabled a multitude of diverse characteristics to

pelled to turn to biological science for their fundamental explanations, classifications and projections,[3] even though relativism assumes at the very outset that culture and cultural differences have no biological basis. Modern relativists cannot escape the dilemma that although as scientists they need categories which are more than mere descriptions of unique behaviour, as relativists they cannot believe that there are any permanent categories.[4]

Relativism as a Methodology

At one time 'relativism' appeared to be a valuable term for classifying those who denied that there were binding norms, as opposed to those who asserted that norms existed. The implied distinction was between non-commitment and commitment, between scepticism and special pleading, between objectivity and subjectivity. The fact that relativists arrived at their position by different routes 're-inforced' the particular arguments they used to establish the relativist position. The various types or 'schools' of relativism were often related to scientific 'facts' which could be marshalled in support of them. Among them, concepts drawn from linguistic analysis, scientific methodology, scepticism, pragmatism, historicism and sociology all combined to make a case for relativism. However, Arnold Brecht's argument in favour of what he calls 'scientific value relativism' raises questions about the nature of relativism and the relation-

[3] Such is the predicament of those who plead for a new, biology-based political theory.

[4] Thus the strict relativist who recognizes the indeterminist element in human behaviour is compelled to see it as Heraclitus saw the universe—a view that makes a 'science' of human behaviour impossible. With the rejection of norms, one abandons the only position between rigid determinism and indeterminate flux which it is possible to take.

---

be brought together under one heading. If a contribution is made by the concept 'sadism', it is not that of ethical neutrality but of discrimination—closer analysis of an already existing normative category, 'cruel behaviour'. One strongly suspects that other 'scientific' concepts which relativists have substituted for the older normative classes are disguised norms. This does not alter the fact that ethically neutral norms are no substitute for values.

ship between the various schools. If a case can be made for scientific value or methodology as a branch of relativism, the whole meaning of relativism must be reconsidered.

To Brecht, 'Scientific Value Relativism is the logical implication of Scientific Method. They are merely two sides of the same thing: the positive and negative side...'[5] According to him, scientific method enables us to investigate a number of questions about normative positions. He lists fifteen of them, but if we analyse the word 'valuable' in terms of purpose—as Brecht does—and also accept his view of a 'complicated interplay between means and purposes',[6] a serious question about the relativist element in scientific methodology arises. 'Scientific value relativism' seems to be a commitment not only to a methodology but also to a methodology as a good.

The charge has long been made, of course, that science recognizes only one good—its own kind of knowledge. But the objection has been considered important only by those who believe there is a kind of good and a kind of knowledge other than that which science reveals. The situation changes, however, as soon as one regards the normative attitude of science as relativist. We can agree that it is relativistic in relation to other norms, but it is obvious that this is not the case as far as its own norms are concerned. To be consistent in their approach, scientists have to regard their own methodology as an absolute: either because it is a good in itself, or because it achieves the kind of knowledge that is a good in itself. Given this fact, exponents of scientific methodology are in no position to analyse other normative views, for we cannot logically begin by saying, in effect, 'Given scientific methodology as an end, or a means to the only end, what can we learn about other ends?' Such a position is tenable from neither the scientific nor relativistic standpoint.

The very use of the term 'relativism', however, reveals a difficulty in the relativist position. We must agree that as a deduction about the nature of norms, relativism is highly plausible, since we cannot 'prove' any of our norms. But as a

[5] Arnold Brecht, *Political Theory: The Foundations of Twentieth-Century Political Thought* (Princeton University Press, 1967), p 118.
[6] *Ibid*, p 121.

methodology, or approach to truth or reality, relativism is absurd. It cannot be a means to anything unless we reduce its meaning to 'scepticism', which would be contrary to the sense in which it is used.

Relativism is an unsuitable basis for a methodology because it denies the binding power of the purpose behind a methodology. When we speak of relativism, we speak of an attitude or belief regarding norms. The nature of this attitude or belief will profoundly affect our approach to normative behaviour, but it cannot itself supply a methodology.

Whatever else relativism may be, it is always in the first place an assumption (before it becomes something else), based possibly on deductions from empirical evidence. The consequences of the assumptions can be analysed by philosophy, but it is not possible to use the assumptions as the basis of a methodology designed to elucidate the nature of norms which are not in keeping with the assumptions. There are different kinds (or schools) of relativism because different assumptions can be made about the nature of norms, each involving types of evidence and lines of reasoning which are virtually independent of all the others. Analyses by the linguistic school, for instance, bear no obvious relation to cultural investigations, even though language has been called pure culture. What is logically excluded is relativism as a methodology: a methodology demands fixity of purpose; a fixed purpose excludes relativism.

Relativity and Relativism

Relativism is not to be confused with relativity. Relativity, strictly defined, means a mathematical space-time theory which has revolutionized cosmology by revising the concept of time and its relation to space. According to Einstein's theory of relativity, positions and events are described in terms of four co-ordinates (in lieu of the traditional three), which are merged in a new space-time entity.

This altered view of time may have caught the popular fancy—it forms the basis of a good deal of science fiction—but it has had no effect on ethical thinking. Advocates of relativism see time, if at all, in the same light as the Utilitarians—as something that can be included in a hedonistic calculus but is of no significance to the norms themselves. Duration is important if the aim is pleasure, but it need not even be mentioned if norms are 'wishes', 'attitudes' and 'tastes'. In this transitory sense the 'norm' may exist only until it is satisfied and then vanish forever: 'time' is irrelevant.

It is the non-relativist conception of norms which—although it antecedes relativity—seems more compatible with the Einsteinian conception of the universe. One of the reasons why the normativist suspects relativist accounts of norms is their failure to incorporate man's sense of the 'reality' of time as an integral part of his normative schemes. What all relativists overlook—especially the hedonist school—is that many of man's norms are negative: they are designed to inhibit and control the impulses and desires which relativists regard as the essential nature of norms. Some religious and all legal sets of norms consist precisely of 'negatives' and there are many people who consider themselves 'moral' purely on the basis of negative action (or inaction): they do not do certain things. Had relativity exercised more influence on ethical thought, this negativism would have received the attention it deserves—it would have been provided with an explanation.

The failure of modern relativism to discuss the time element is particularly striking when we consider that the modern physicist's conception of the universe includes time as an essential part; the same attitude with regard to norms could provide a better empirical description of norms and a better philosophic understanding of normative behaviour. A primary difference between a desire (or taste) and a 'norm' is that the latter has a place in a time scheme whereas the former does not. Inhibitions—considered as part of a normative scheme—are explicable not only in terms of the rest of the normative set but also of man's position in time. Without the individual's sense of duration in time, norms cannot be understood.

Hedonists err by seeing time in relation to norms in the same way as the classical physicists did—as something belonging to the 'reality' of space but as not being directly related to it.

Consequently, hedonists produce a confusing calculus which requires that considerations of time be opposed to those of intensity and so forth; time is regarded as one of many independent factors rather than as an integral part of norms. If relativity—like relativism—were really part of our view of the world, it ought to have made us aware that the very sense of self on which hedonism is based requires us to view the self in time—and hence to see time as an integral part of any normative scheme. But modern ethical analyses have not attempted to make time as important as self, and inseparable from it. Clearly, then, relativity has not affected relativism. Indeed, relativism in the forms known to us, would probably vanish if relativity were to play any part in relativist analysis.

To conclude: relativity and relativism are not interchangeable. Both are science-induced: but while relativity is a 'primary' scientific concept, relativism is a derived (or 'second-generation') formulation: it has gone beyond scientific thinking and permeated social consciousness. Both are universal (although different types of universality apply to them): the universal, extra-terrestrial validity of the theory of relativity has not yet been disproved; relativism, on the other hand, is an assumption, a point of view, an attitude, a pseudo-ideology, whose ubiquitous—though essentially earthbound—nature has still to be fully revealed.

Relativism and Political Science

A problem for political science is the need to distinguish between approaching society from a relativist point of view and studying society as if it were relativist *per se*. These positions are different and lead to different results. Thus a relativistically inclined political scientist avoids traditional political theory, since the analysis of logical consequences of ideas and normative manipulation which characterize that theory seem to him but a reflection of the normative thinking of the investigator himself. According to the relativist, the nature of norms is such that what influences one man need not necessarily influence others. This would of course be true if all men were genuine relativists, which is not the case. Although most people are technically relativists (supporting laws they recognize as subject to change, advocating strict majority rule, etc) they look on their relativistically-based norms as absolutes. This is a state of affairs that has persisted throughout history and whose recognition can lead to a form of relativism (a form, however, without a philosophic basis: all that it assumes is that some of the 'absolutes' in which men believe are not really absolutes). What the relativist must keep in mind—no matter how he arrived at his relativism—is that whether norms are in fact all relativist at their base or not, there are conditions in every society which allow political theory to work, even though they 'should not' (according to him) do so. Too often the views of the relativist affect his methodology: he acts as if the known facts about norms in society were not facts. He 'idealizes' conditions by pretending that members of society are relativists in the philosophic sense. Thus he eliminates some crucial facts of contemporary political orders—the normative basis of ideologies—and focusses his attention on institutional and behaviouralistic aspects, which are, of course, unintelligible outside their ideological context.[7]

Is a relativist bound to assume that he is studying only relativist phenomena, or can he recognize that it is he, not the theorist, whose initial position does not reflect the views of those he is studying? Can he adjust his position accordingly? There are no logical reasons for him not to do so. He should be able to recognize that relativism places the political scientist in the same predicament as atheism puts those who study Christianity. The situation has both its advantages and disadvantages; the moment, however, when the intellectual stance is 'projected' onto the object of study as if everyone held it, the study becomes worthless. A philosophic relativist would

---

[7] It is rather like studying rats in a maze, while beginning with the assumption that under no circumstances can one suppose that they are trying to get out of the maze or follow any other purposeful behaviour. All sorts of interesting observations can be made, but the initial assumption makes it impossible to understand them.

presumably know this and be careful to avoid projecting his beliefs or letting them guide his methodology: there should be no connection between relativism and methodology. But the political scientist's practice belies this principle—as in the relativist 'idealization' of society—and suggests that other factors besides relativism are at work.

Relativism and the Hierarchy of Values

Every government, whether society is relativist or not, must face the problem of priorities. Few, if any, governments today can act as if they had an administrative function only, and—like an ideal bureaucracy—assign tasks to the correct department and let the machinery of bureaucracy cope with them. A democratic government is in a peculiarly difficult position. It cannot be wholeheartedly relativist (as democratic theory requires); even if it believes that such is its function, it cannot assign priorities according to the apparent strength of the demand for action. The community's wishes have no order. To become policy, they must be ordered in terms of some concept of importance which is not inherent in them.

Relativists among the public (hardly any of whom recognize themselves as such) insist that demands on governments do order themselves in terms of strength: the strength of numbers ('most people want . . .') or the strength of self-interest ('those most affected want . . .'). But this kind of ordering of demands cannot serve the policy-maker who must establish priorities among conflicting demands arising from different kinds of 'strength'. Black power members, environmentalist groups, women's liberation fronts and others may suppose that what has priority is self-evident: they strive to increase their show of strength in order to guarantee that their goals obtain priority in this way. But their activity only makes the policy-maker's decisions more difficult: his attention has to be diverted from long-range policy goals to their daily demands, and to maintaining law and order. The problem of priorities is made worse—not easier—by insistent pressures.

Through being forced to focus on law and order questions, the modern administrator is moving back to the hierarchy of values established by that early 'relativist', Hobbes, who recognized that traditional natural law is much too individualistic and personal to serve man in society. Hobbes' position was that if you are to focus on the problem of justice and order in this world, the first necessity is a system of 'natural law' whose principal characteristic is that it has a supreme norm and not simply a supreme law-giver, as in theological conceptions. (It is because of this major shift in normative thinking that those who consider the concept of sovereignty as the application to society of a theological conception of the universe are quite mistaken.) Hobbes' supreme law-giver is 'supreme' only so long as he operates within the hierarchy of values which make him supreme. (Thus, in a sense, Hobbes was also an anti-relativist.) If he attempts to behave as a relativist—a temporal god capable of ordering society according to his will as God orders the universe—he abandons the normative order which gives him the authority to be anything other than an equal among equals. It is not in his interest to do this—and probably not within his ability to do it rationally or consciously. Although the sovereign is not a party to the social contract, he is, apparently, a party to the normative code which underlies the social contract concept. Hobbes represents his hierarchy of norms as one 'natural to' a rational being.

We tend today to regard Hobbes' analysis of 'natural law' as based on too narrow a conception of self, and as a result we minimize its major contribution—the idea of a hierarchy of values without which we might add, we have either anarchy or tyranny. The misfortune imposed by modern relativism is that it presents the problem of society as an attempt to find a balance between the two alternatives. Relativism since Hobbes has thought of norms purely as sets of desires which have no order and are by nature incapable of any 'natural' or 'rational' order, so that such order as exists must always be imposed. Presumably, each man decides for himself just how much 'freedom' he is willing to give up, and each government makes a guess as to how much 'order' it can impose. It seems an unsatisfactory way of analysing political order.

What is then the problem with relativism as an assumption on which to base an analysis of society? It is that the absence of order in values (entailed by relativism) requires us to analyse society in terms of two alternatives, anarchy v tyranny—the position that uninformed critics of Hobbes have first represented as his view and then shown to be untenable. It is untenable because it is wrong to represent all governments as varying forms of tyranny and all communities without formal political order as living in a state of nature. Hobbes never implied that such was the case. Though he began with relativist assumptions, he recognized that those assumptions do not in themselves allow us to describe actual conditions anywhere.

Modern relativism has never moved beyond Hobbes' initial assumption; instead it has proceeded to analyse society on the basis of it alone. As a result, we are expected to understand political activity as a form of the power struggle Hobbes saw in the 'state of nature', but deprived of the rational element—the ordering of choices—which Hobbes considered necessary to power struggles. To get around the difficulty that desires must either be rationally ordered into norms when they cannot immediately be achieved, or else abandoned, relativists have invented a special desire for man called 'power-hunger', which has been established as the true basis of political activity. In consequence, political activity is now represented as power-hunger operating within sets of social restrictions, such as the law and forms of political organization.

Such an approach makes nonsense of all traditional concepts of political theory. It is interesting to note that the dispute does not arise from the theorist's desire to use classical concepts, but from his analysis of political orders. This is so, because pure relativism requires us to make assumptions contrary to plain facts. Hobbes saw this centuries ago: the 'state of nature' is *not* a fact; the tyranny of law is *not* a fact; man versus society is *not* a fact. Hobbes moved beyond relativism as we know it today not because he had a speculative mind, but because relativism is quite unable to describe the world as we see it and unable to account for what we see. By going beyond relativism, Hobbes compels us to reappraise it. Modern relativists will have to establish that each step Hobbes took beyond pure relativism was completely unnecessary. Otherwise, they will have to show evidence of an actual 'state of nature' in the world today. Their very inability to do so must expose the fallacy of relativist assumptions.

The modern normativist differs from the relativist primarily because he insists that normative behaviour is not to be understood merely as the choice between means and ends but as the ordering of ends—creating a hierarchy of norms. But very few normativists today focus on questions of proving or disproving that a particular norm is a 'natural law' norm. Today, almost everyone is to some extent a relativist, believing there is nothing in the arrangement of the universe that compels man to have his present norms. Rather the problem is which norms can be fitted into a pattern that permits us to behave in the way we want.

The relativist would argue that we always behave as we wish, except when coerced by circumstances. For him, 'freedom' means the elimination of impediments to the fulfilment of our desires. He equates having 'power' with freedom to act according to desire. Thus, a judge who announces that he dislikes having to make a particular decision but is compelled by his sense of the common good to make it, is said to be a hypocrite.[8]

The desire for power becomes a desire for freedom—the condition in which we can achieve our desires. It is implied that we are all in a Hobbesian state of nature, except that we do not order our desires as Hobbes envisaged. This view of human behaviour makes society and political order unintelligible. It is an anarchistic view that fails the first test of any such conjecture about behaviour: it cannot move logically from the hypothetic disorder of human desires to the actual social orders. If we wish to begin with a Hobbesian hypothesis about man's desires—a position forced on us by modern philosophic

---

[8] It is this attitude towards those wielding power which leads to the immense suspicion of authority today. Action such as that taken by the Canadian Government against the FLQ in 1970 is not seen as a reluctant and temporary infringement of democratic norms, but as an opportunistic extension of power revealing the norms ('desires') of those in a position to do what they want.

relativism—we have, as Hobbes did, to supplement the hypothesis with a system ordering our desires. We have to fit our conjectures into the known facts of social order; we cannot presuppose both anarchistic individualism and social order.

The failure of political theorists to build upon Hobbes' theory is understandable. Traditionally, his conjectures about normative thinking have seemed cynical and his analysis of the State a plea for absolutism. Liberal democrats, especially, have resisted the Hobbesian argument. But while controversies about the validity of the theory have been raging, relativism has been breaking down the order of values we inherited. The norms themselves are of course still present. When we say that the normative order is breaking down, we do not mean that people now believe property norms to be meaningless or that the 'puritan ethic' is for Puritans only. Rather, we speak of bizarre shifts in the normative order. Thus the great majority of people, including the violent, still disapprove of violence, but it is no longer clear what occasions make it tolerable as an expedient. There are some naïve 'absolutists' who pretend there are never any exceptions to norms. They deny, in reality, that norms form a hierarchy; they are relativists with an authoritarian bent. That this simplicist absolutism can be regarded—as it often is—as an alternative to relativism is due to the fact that we have grown unaccustomed to normative analysis. The Sunday sermons which once helped us to order our norms no longer serve any large body of citizens. The central norms of our society now derive from the State rather than the Church, but the State does not have any system of ordering norms; it pretends that the family and Church still serve that function. The point has now been reached where the State must begin to reappraise its position. It must be remembered that norms are still with us, but—being 'unordered'—they contribute to our aimless behaviour. We are relativists only in the sense that our norms are disordered. The consequences for the State and society are serious, and political theory faces pressing responsibilities.

The Consequences of Scientism

Scientism has functioned primarily as a negative force by raising doubts about political theory and by exposing the limitations of normative categories. In our age it would be natural to expect scientism to have profoundly influenced political theory since it insists that the theorist's norms—his 'data'—must have precisely the characteristics which he attributes to them. The theorist, of course, is not able to achieve this. His assumptions about human behaviour reintroduce the concept of purpose which scientific method has abandoned as untestable; and he orders his concepts into rational patterns despite persistent attempts by the empiricists to show that mankind does not behave rationally. Worse still, he has to hypostatize abstractions such as the 'State', the 'Nation', the 'Law', and the 'Constitution' in situations where the scientist can find only people and groups of people. When the theorist says 'The State must...', the scientist translates this as 'The theorist wants people to...'. Despite its trenchant criticisms, however, scientism has not produced anything remotely resembling a substitute for political theory.

The principal reason why scientism has had little effect on theory is that the methods of the theorist and those of the scientist are incompatible with one another. Even if both agreed that certain basic concepts—such as equality and individualism—are meaningful and have some validity, the 'scientistically'-oriented would object to the theorist's supposition that the intellectual manipulation of norms, and suggesting ways of avoiding rational difficulties and institutional problems in expressing norms, are valid. For the 'scientistically'-oriented the results could only reflect the particular theorist's mental processes and normative patterns. They would have no necessary relation to those of other persons and hence —unless the theorist sought to impose them on others—no significance for society. For the theorist, on the other hand, norms and theorizing about them are closely related. If norms by definition represent goals for which man consciously strives, then rational analysis of the difficulties involved in integrating and institutionalizing them will reflect the direction in which society is moving. What the theorist concludes from his study gives an advance indication of what society will probably do in the long run.

Scientism has shown that it cannot supply tools which parallel those of the theorist or do anything approaching his work. Yet, although it has had very little direct impact on theory, it has affected the latter indirectly. Many of those who might have entered the field of theory have opted for behaviouralism. The doubts that scientism raises about tools and methods induce most analysts to choose what seems to be science, in preference to what seems to be mere armchair philosophy. This is reinforced by the preference of those who employ political scientists for their 'practical' knowledge, as contrasted with the 'impracticable' theory of political philosophers. Since the advice given by political scientists—usually behaviouralists—necessarily involves normative judgements, the results have not been impressive. This is because the behaviouralist—unlike the theorist—has not been compelled to analyse his own norms.

Both the behaviouralist and society insist on relativism—a fact that is made clear by the close relationship between what the behaviouralist undertakes to investigate and the conditions which society defines as problems to be solved. The behaviouralist is much closer to being a servant of his society than the physicist or chemist. The physical scientist's major problems are set by the theories his discipline has evolved; even those scientists whose specific investigations are set by society derive a sense of prestige from the discipline's independence of society. Theoretically, the physicist works for 'science': he adds to its body of knowledge. The social scientist cannot pretend to do anything more than study situations created by a society—in most cases, his own. For him, the assertion of independence can take one form only—the 'expert' must determine policy. He is, of course, in no position to do this if he has accepted norms with any kind of absolute validity. Such norms would parallel the objective 'truths' of the physicist, except that, once found, they would (by the nature of absolute norms) bind the investigator. Conceivably, the investigator might have to give up further studies in order to prove by his own behaviour that his norms were indeed what he represented them to be. The

Church's historical hostility to science was based on similar reasoning. Scientific investigation was not a 'Christian' pursuit: Christian norms required a different type of behaviour. Our society makes no such assertion, but if the social scientist is to achieve an independence similar to that of the physicist, then his claim to the pursuit of 'truth' and 'knowledge' must be replaced by an assertion of the validity of relativism. Relativism alone supplies him with freedom of action (necessary to pursue his investigations) which demands respect. For the social sciences, the stance of scientific objectivity has to take the form of relativism. For the physical scientist, on the other hand, 'objectivity' means that to the best of his ability he will avoid introducing irrelevant norms into his investigations.

This need to assert independence in an area where dependence appears to be the usual condition is reinforced by the empirically-minded social scientist's desire to enlarge the significance of his studies. Even a trivial fact discovered by a physical scientist adds to our body of knowledge and is therefore of value, but this does not hold true if the 'fact' is about a unique situation, as most—perhaps all—behaviouralist studies are. Only if the behaviouralist is allowed also to determine how the fact is to be fitted into a normative scheme of what is important and unimportant, useful or not, can he gain the physical scientist's prestige. The very nature of his studies makes him want to believe in government by the 'expert'. This is why we have today so many proposals for such government. Governments have of course always relied on the advice of those with specialized knowledge. Proposals for the greater use of experts have become not so much arguments for the substitution of informed opinion for arbitrary fiats, as hidden arguments for the supposition that an 'is' can and should become an 'ought'. (To interpret the 'ought' as if it were an 'is' can only result in nonsense. We would expect science to stop short when confronted with the view that 'is' and 'ought' differ; also that science—being designed to deal only with the 'is'—can say nothing about the 'ought'. Its only possible contribution would be a catalogue of 'oughts'!)

For the social scientist the normative 'ought' imposes a serious limitation not only on the ease with which he conducts his investigations but on the worth of their results. As regards normative statements, he is in the same position as Galileo when the Church told him what was possible and useful. It is not surprising, therefore, that the social scientist tends to regard himself as a latter day Galileo defending the truth against arbitrary authority. But, instead of being able to point to the evidence of what actually is the case, he must assert his own authority. It is he who must refuse to investigate further the problems forced upon him by his position of 'expert' in a relativistic society. Just as the physical scientist in the days of theological authoritarianism had to cling firmly to the view that knowledge of the truths of physical science was an intrinsic good, so the social scientist must claim that relativism is an intrinsic good, no matter how bizarre it is philosophically.

Is an 'Empirically-Based Theory' Possible?

To be successful, an empirical approach in the social sciences needs a (non-empirical) faith in the appropriateness of the methodology. One should remember that more than a century of sustained effort by thousands of investigators has failed to produce a single law of human behaviour comparable to the physical laws formulated during the infancy of scientific method. That human behaviour is more complex than that studied by the physical sciences, is a fact that can be empirically observed and can lead to still greater effort and more complex techniques of analysis. The real problem for the empiricist—the reason why he must develop a faith—is that an empirically-based theory in the social sciences can describe only the particular phenomena from which it was derived. Thus the voting behaviour of blue-collar workers in a New Jersey suburb in November 1972 describes this behaviour alone. If it appeared to do more, to be evidence of a law of blue-collar voting, the empiricist would be the first to recognize that his investigations had gone astray; for empiricism certainly suggests that human behaviour is not determined by wearing a blue collar or having a certain level of intelligence. There is no evidence that any given conditions in man invariably lead to given behaviour. Even experimentally-induced conditioned responses—which achieve spectacular results in animals—work consistently only among very young human beings.

The empiricist, then, must resort to an act of faith to continue his investigations. He must say that, despite evidence to the contrary, he will affirm that choice is an illusion, and that man is bound as tightly in a chain of cause and effect as the universe was believed to be, by some eighteenth century theorists.

From this act of faith it follows that the real reason for the failure of empiricism in the social sciences is the complexity of subject-matter and the difficulty of distinguishing the multiple causes behind even the simplest human behaviour. It also follows that what the investigator needs is a larger number of investigations—a particularly popular plea among behaviouralists of various schools—and more refined tools of analysis: bigger computers to process data; more complex surveys; and more ingenious methods of overcoming the difficulties of investigating phenomena that are capable of recognizing they are being investigated and of altering their behaviour accordingly.

Is the empiricist's 'faith' justifiable? It was understandable when the cause-effect premise of science was considered inviolable. The introduction of choice into such a system would, of course, place the social sciences in a special category having no clear relation to the rest of science but some affinities with the theological conception of the universe (which proved hostile to all science). Indeterminism makes it now less obvious why empiricists should attempt to establish an empirically-based theory in the social sciences. Yet the alternative to empiricism in the social sciences does not even have an adequate name. To talk about it, we must invent one: for example, normativism.

The two approaches are by no means sharply separated. The normativist bases his approach on what empiricism cannot avoid revealing: that human behaviour is goal-directed rather than 'caused', and that the goals—or norms—are put into 'rational', orderly patterns that do not necessarily resemble the patterns from which they were derived. From the assumption—

based on excellent empirical evidence—that the patterns formed by the individual are almost always orderly, it follows that an observer—given some of the norms—can predict some of the patterns, and—by himself manipulating the norms—can foresee the consequences to both the individual and society, if certain norms are accepted.

Empiricism does not discredit the normativist's assumption about normative patterns. Indeed, many attempts to refine empirical methodology are based on the same assumption. Both the empiricist and the normativist believe that if a man holds the 'freedom of speech' norm, he will, other factors being equal, uphold the 'right' of a dissenter to express himself. What they do, if this proves untrue, shows the essential difference in their approach. The empiricist returns to his field studies and by manipulating his techniques attempts to discover what the man's norm 'really' is, or perhaps tries to find the factors that made his respondent say he believed in the norm when in fact he did not. The empiricist's very methodology leads him to the belief that he must either refine his technique or give up the belief that normative statements have any impact on behaviour. Paradoxically it is the normativist who remains much closer to what empirical observation shows—that it is perfectly possible for a man to assert a norm and then fail to observe all its requirements. Instead of assuming that a mistake was made during observation, he attempts to conceive a normative pattern that will accommodate the apparent discrepancy.

Even a 'strict' empiricist—who is not likely to be as strict as he pretends—will probably not deny the influence of normative patterns. (His major problem is to prevent just such an influence while he is obtaining his data.) Yet it is clear from the lack of empirical studies of normative patterns in both individuals and societies that the empiricist is hostile to normative approaches and avoids them.

In the physical sciences empiricism has played a major rôle in theoretical development, but it has never been the sole basis for theory, as the narrower thesis of empiricism maintains. Even such scientific laws as Boyle's or Gay-Lussac's—which seem no more than empirically observed regularities—are not mere generalized descriptions: they require the concept of an 'ideal'—imaginary—gas. The recognition that a regularity or law has in effect been imposed may help to explain the tendency toward an empirically-based theory in the social sciences. The question that keeps arising is: Might there not be, beneath the great diversity of human behaviour, the same kind of regularities which will become observable when suitable methods of observation have been developed?

The hypothesis that such regularities exist obviously influences empiricists in the social sciences, but the resulting activity is unlike efforts in the physical sciences—it requires presuppositions about the results that have never been present in empirical investigations of the physical world. In the first place, physical sciences began with observable regularities which they made universal through the concept of the ideal. They did not have to assume that the regularities were there. Consequently, even highly abstract mathematical formulations in the physical sciences are largely reducible to empirical observations (of which some—perhaps most—have not yet been made). Now if we change the method by searching for the regularities instead of starting with them, we are bound to make assumptions about the nature of what we are investigating that must affect our results.

Thus the assumption that there are uniformities beneath cultural and individual diversity—man being a member of the species homo sapiens—is necessarily an assumption about the influence of biology upon society. Conjectures about the rôle of sex, aggression, territorial imperatives and so forth are widely accepted, even though empirical observation of their rôle is not possible. Diverse phenomena are conjectured to be manifestations of sex, or some other drive, not on the basis of empirical observation of regularities but on the assumption that divergent behaviour must have a regularity which is an aspect of the only possible one—the biological nature of man. Needless to say, this kind of hypothesis is not testable, for the regularity which permits experiment, prediction and testing in the physical sciences is not present in the social science hypothesis. Where the behaviour of gas A, B and C under set conditions gives rise to a statement that will be changed if the regularity is not always observable, the regularity in the social sciences *is* the hypothesis—not the source of it.

Most social scientists avoid the difficulties present in theories of behaviour based on assumed regularities by eschewing theory and searching for regularities which—when discovered—will presumably permit genuine theory: facts first, then theory. Without realizing it, however, they adopt the narrower thesis of empiricism, the supposition that the entire science can be reduced to empirical observation. This, of course, cannot be done. In order to have a theory one must have a selective principle concerning empirical observations, or an assumption about possible relations. The physical sciences have always acted this way. They could never have developed if they had first to search for the regularities: the possibilities are theoretically infinite.[9]

The empiricists' sense of hopelessness is in part related to the close connection between most social science studies and the goals set by society. The bulk of social science is now directed by the requirements of social policy in the society in which it takes place—it is 'practical' rather than theoretical. There is no shame in this. Social scientists are not being venal when by their studies they supply information about voting behaviour and factors in race riots. The fact remains that they are not capable of developing any useful theory from such studies, for the 'problem' they investigate is set and defined by social norms, not by 'facts' in the usual sense.

A most serious limitation of pure empiricism is its inability to deal adequately with normative behaviour: empirically-based analyses of the latter do not allow us to draw any conclusions. Thus statistics can show that at certain times and places certain people may do both X and Y. But if such facts are to attain significance, we have to know what the relation between X and Y is. But there is nothing that compels us to believe that a relation must exist. Furthermore, in view of the nature of normative 'exceptions'—which are expressions of interactions between norms—or 'inconsistencies', the significance of the re-

---

[9] Without a theory based on observable regularities, it is plausible to conjecture that the song of Siamese jungle birds is related to the use of birth control pills in Canada or that American foreign policy is influenced by the presence of mammoth skeletons in Alaska.

lations will vary according to the normative sets that are accepted. Conceivably, a highly elaborate system of empirical studies could give some idea about the relations between the Xs and Ys of normative behaviour, but it is hard to envisage how such studies could distinguish between what a normativist would regard as a logical inconsistency—which could be corrected by pointing it out (or so normativists believe)—and what would be an exception, namely the operation of another norm—which cannot be corrected by pointing to it.

This major difference in the response to what the observer regards as an inconsistency has given added weight to relativistic arguments. The relativists assume that—because people do not usually change their behaviour when 'inconsistencies' are pointed out—normative behaviour is not 'logical' and cannot be studied by logical analysis: all political theorizing is a waste of time. The normativist's answer is that because only logical analysis is able to distinguish between 'inconsistency' and 'exception', it alone can deal with normative behaviour. Although empirical analyses of political behaviour may yield conclusions that permit action, those conclusions are themselves based on something other than empiricism. Furthermore, because they almost inevitably confuse elementary distinctions that are self-evident to the theorist, the recommendations of the empiricist can be misleading and even dangerous to society.

The relativist, committed to the view that norms are expressions of tastes, attitudes and desires, is necessarily committed to a single way of interpreting evidence of 'inconsistencies' in normative behaviour and to dwell on this as if it were the only evidence. The fact that a very large number of people—perhaps the majority—believe both that killing is wrong and capital punishment is right, is for him further evidence that normative statements are not 'rational' and that it is futile to debate them. Logically—he argues—anyone holding the view that the killing of a human being is wrong must claim that capital punishment is wrong. He is led to this interpretation because he is committed to the non-rationality of normative behaviour. The normativist can interpret things differently: he is not committed to excluding evidence. He recognizes that in fact some people are open to the argument that 'logically' the man who disapproves of killing must disapprove of capital punishment. There is clear evidence in recent developments in the criminal law that some men at least have changed their normative position to accord with their view. But to the relativists this is difficult to explain; any change in norms is mysterious to them and so is the communication of norms within society and the continuance of any normative patterns.

But if the normativist is able to explain why men change—or appear to change—their normative position when inconsistencies in their behaviour are pointed out, what can he do about the large number of people who do not change their position? What about those who resisted, and still object to, the abolition of capital punishment? Do they have norms which are different from those held by persons who welcomed the elimination of an 'inconsistency'? Is the relativist right in the sense that men in general disregard inconsistencies because most normative sets have no logical requirement? The normativist adopts the view that anything that maintains an historical continuity should find a logical place in a social scheme which pretends to explain or even describe. He does not believe that 'inconsistencies' are illogical. He can perceive them as quite logical exceptions, the result of an interaction between norms in which the 'exception' indicates the presence of a norm having a higher position on some normative scale. It is in fact quite easy to regard the concept of capital punishment as a logical exception to the norm about killing, if one recognizes that the concept of sovereignty is implicitly present in the mind of the general public.

Computer-Made Theory, Experimental Ideologies and 'Instant' Systems

What if empiricism had its way? What future would it hold for political theory? Empiricists hope that 'their' theory will be a guide to action. I prefer to see their theory as a contribution to inaction. Thus we can envisage life itself as one huge experimental field for a games theory. Instead of applying the latter to some life-situations—which is its task at present—in order to clarify them and foresee the implications of various alternatives, life can be imagined as serving the purpose of testing the games theory and other theories that are likely to emerge.

Strategic staff games played by the Pentagon officers and RAND experts have been known to create their own rules and limitations and impose rigid demands on those engaged in them. Perhaps the day is not far off when these bloodless wars will become a substitute for real war. Conceivably, they may also become substitutes for other types of activity: business transactions, financial speculations, politicking, sports, social 'upmanship' etc. Ultimately, game-playing may become a substitute for living as we know it today: all human action will be make-believe. Game-playing will offer a whole range of emotions—satisfactions and frustrations—which otherwise may not be given to an individual in a life-time. And since playing —unlike real life activity—will spare the player dangerous or unpleasant consequences, it will increase his propensity to play —it will create a lifelong addiction.

The tyranny of that age will be absolute and moral disintegration complete. Principles and standards will be but 'rules of the game' that one adopts for the purpose of a particular game only. With a complete absence of a moral consensus on standards, values will be no more than semantic labels, changed at will, shuffled at will to produce the desirable mix and attached at will to a particular set of circumstances required by the game. Political theory will become a super-set of rules which are applicable to a situation desirable for a particular lifegame and can be duly programmed into a computer. Hence, anything that cannot be programmed will no longer qualify as theory.

Computerized game-playing—as a substitute for 'living'—will not be limited to games whose basic rules are already known and which simply call for decisions in answer to the alternatives with which the player has been confronted by the computer. The next, and inevitable, step will be to use the computer to create new rules of the game, by programming into it the ingredients of rules, or various sets of rules—values, as it were—with the help of which not only new rules but also new games can be 'invented'. In the socio-political realm this will offer the dazzling possibilities of creating experimental ideologies, hitherto practised in only a relatively limited fashion by totalitarian countries. But whereas in 'traditional' totalitarian systems any experimentation had the inevitable drawback of being slow in inception, cumbersome in application and uncertain of results,[10] computerized experimentation will provide the possibility of rapid testing and general availability of experience through 'participation' in 'instant' systems.

Can Philosophy and Science be Reconciled?

Historically, science evolved from philosophy, but it later developed such a huge body of knowledge—some of it not obviously reconcilable with philosophy—that the achievement of a compatible relationship between the two now appears doubtful. At one time, science was a branch of philosophy and its discoveries had to be fitted into the rational patterns of the older discipline. Empirical observations were expected to 'make sense'. This is no longer true. The current theory of light, for instance, may accord well with empirical observations, but not fit into a rational or intelligible pattern. The breach between the two disciplines has widened: the fact that some scientific facts are intelligible only as empirical observations, has strengthened the conviction of those in the social sciences who insist that *only* empirical observations make sense. In their eyes, there is no place for philosophy.

The paradoxical feature of science is that by justifying itself as empiricism it becomes less empirical and ends as a pseudo-philosophy of empiricism making extravagant claims to universality. How else did science enter the field of ethics? Countering the philosophic argument that it is logically impossible to move

---

[10] Thus, by not being easily available to those outside the system, it tended to create in the minds of some 'liberals' ambivalent (or even downright 'fellow-travelling') feelings as to its desirability.

from 'is' to 'ought', the relativist scientist claims that the 'is' is the 'ought'! He can give no empirical evidence for this: he can only supply facts. But facts are not evidence unless fitted into a non-factual, non-empirical pattern—until they mean something more than their mere sum. Here is the crux of the problem: science has grown so independent of its mother-discipline that it refuses to acknowledge that its 'problems' and patterns are not self-generated.

Must the social scientist arrogate to himself the tasks of philosophy? The forces moving men in this direction are strong, but it is absurd for the behaviouralist to undertake the task he is pursuing. That we need statistics, field studies and questionnaires about human behaviour cannot be denied: they are the stuff of empirical investigations. But to imagine that such investigations can direct themselves—that they should be undertaken simply because observations are possible—is sheer madness. Their purpose must ultimately be determined by non-empirical philosophical considerations. The question is: will this happen, thereby bringing about a reconciliation of science and philosophy? It is unlikely that the required change of attitude will occur until there is a change in our society's attitude to reason. As men are not required to make full use of reason, it is conceivable that some of the intellectual absurdities of modern social science are forced upon the protagonists by the mere fact of living in a society. If they were not, we would expect some ingenious and adroit defences of modern scientism and behaviouralism. But these are absent: scientism and behaviouralism are 'facts' rather than theories.

Scientism and behaviouralism are also philosophic abberrations. It is the failure of modern philosophy that forces the social scientist into an untenable philosophical position. He is required to analyse human behaviour by a method which—as he understands it—cannot yield the same results as it does in the physical world. He cannot ascribe to empirical observations a secondary rather than a primary role, because he knows that human behaviour differs from the interactions of chemicals or physical forces; he cannot logically abandon or even modify his empiricism on the basic of empirical evidence. It is for someone else—the philosopher—to deal with the very difficult problem posed by the philosophic need—perhaps only 'desire'—for one kind of truth attained by a single method and the fact that this method supplies evidence that either there is another truth or that an additional method is required. It is unreasonable to expect the social scientist to suspend operations until this problem is solved, or to expect him to invent a new methodology to deal with the peculiar problems of human behaviour.

The failure of scientism and behaviouralism are the failures of philosophy which—in the last analysis—are imposed by society. Philosophy is, of course, not doomed forever to play its present subordinate rôle, although the importance of rôles is decided by society. In our case, a major emphasis has long ago been placed on man's manipulation of the physical world and hence on science. Man's own behaviour—and its directions—formerly seemed to be adequately covered by society's normative order. The early years of modern democracy were years of a normative order and hence a considerable importance was given to philosophy. But the rise of relativism left little room for philosophy. For many years now the philosopher—and the historian—have had nothing important to say to society: their rôle has been one of minor importance.

It is possible that the socially awkward consequences of relativism will in the future restore the importance of philosophy and thereby end the philosophic impasse facing the social scientist. Relativism makes the normative order—which is the logical foundation of a society—a purely arbitrary imposition by society. Under this scheme law and order go together because order *is* law. It is an absurd position for our society to accept. Few people really want to believe it. Most advocates of law and order do not profess to believe that the law is merely the law; they want the law to be an expression of a universal normative order. Yet their position is enforced by relativism, or rather the conflicting relativisms induced by science and philosophy, and inherent in egalitarianism. We would have no problem if our relativisms produced a single attitude toward norms; as they do not, we cannot achieve even the logical relativist attitude to norms. (We have, in fact, a system of unrestrained, utterly chaotic relativisms.) As relativists, we should be able to ignore norms, accept them or shift our attitude toward them according to our mood. Science, of course, has nothing to say about what the attitude 'should' be. It is for philosophy to make new pronouncements, since society is beginning again to ask for them. Society is now changing its attitude to the question of the reconciliation of philosophy and science, in that it is no longer being assumed that satisfactory solutions to the problem of human behaviour will come from science.

The Consequences of Behaviouralism

Are we perhaps at the threshold of a new era in which behaviouralism will be transformed into something else? How plausible is 'post-behaviouralism'—the concept put forward in 1969 by David Easton? Is his 'post-behaviouralism' a school of thought that could replace behaviouralism, or is it rather a set of objections to the latter? If—following Easton—we accept the 'tenets' of this new current, we are likely to believe that it is a mass of discordant opinions, of which even the exact number is difficult to determine. The number of 'tenets' given by Easton is seven—an apparently arbitrary number, for it is difficult to understand why it should be preferred to, say, two.[11] Easton admits that no single post-behaviouralist would hold all these views—a fact which, particularly if taken together with the unsystematic nature of the 'tenets', raises the question whether the future trend is simply a catch-all term for various unrelated criticisms of behaviouralism.

[11] Considering both the formulation and the subsequent discussion of the issues raised, the seven points can be paraphrased as follows: (1) clear-cut, normative commitment is preferable to clear description, though the two may not be opposed; (2) behaviouralism is unwittingly committed to social conservativism; (3) behaviouralism avoids commitment; (4) commitment is inevitable and must be conscious; (5) commitment should be to 'humane values'; (6) knowledge requires commitment and activism; (7) groups of scholars as well as individuals should be committed. See: David Easton, 'The New Revolution in Political Science', *The American Political Science Review*, LXIII, No 4, December 1969, pp 1051–61.

Highly significant is Easton's concession that behaviouralists are normatively committed and that he considers it important that they be aware of their commitment. (This is precisely the concession that non-behaviouralists have always wanted from this school!) The essence of Easton's argument is that the addition of normative awareness to the behaviouralist methodology will be an important new development. But the existing anti-normative bias makes it impossible for behaviouralism to analyse normative situations and is the most crucial shortcoming of the school—the reason why the latter never deals adequately with the full 'facts' of political behaviour. Thus, committed methodologically to a denial of norms, 'post-behaviouralism' will be in no position to incorporate norms at any point in the future. Perhaps nothing called 'post-behaviouralism' can ever evolve from the present methodology. In the final analysis, it appears that Easton is not talking of a potential logical development in political theory or scientific methodology, but making a minimum concession to the critics of behaviouralism.

Furthermore, 'post-behaviouralism' cannot—as Easton implies—be both a new trend and an extension of behaviouralism. Although he sees the need for something new that will go beyond behaviouralism, it is apparent from what he says of the 'success' of behaviouralism that for him future developments in political science will be merely extensions of the behaviouralist approach. He asserts that behaviouralism has shifted political science from prescription, ethical enquiry and action to description, explanation and verification, and that one cannot deny the growing success of behaviouralist endeavours. He sees the future in terms of prescription, ethical enquiry and action being superimposed on the current description, explanation and verification of behaviouralism.

What are the weaknesses of this analysis? The non-behaviouralist can have no serious quarrel with such objectives, but he denies of course that behaviouralists have been as successful as Easton maintains. Since behaviouralists describe unique events, verification in the usual scientific sense is impossible, and 'explanation' becomes another kind of description—a description of some concomitants of the events studied. Close attention to all the circumstances of given situations has enabled the physical sciences to employ the concept of causation to arrive at what are regarded as genuine explanations of the factors that 'cause' certain phenomena. But we cannot do this with impunity in respect of human behaviour. If we do, the methodology used produces some curious effects on our thinking.

One of the major effects of behaviouralism is that it forces us to look at human behaviour in a non-rational light: human reasons and purposes cannot by its methodology be separated from the non-rational. Thus in behavioural studies residence and occupation—utterly 'non-rational' elements—are presented as if they were of major importance. They are made to seem so because they can be easily investigated as factors, whereas reasons and purposes cannot.

With this downgrading of the rational, the attitude to norms is changed: they are considered arbitrary and conventional. In this context ideology and ideological analysis lose all significance.

As a result of its non rationality, behaviouralist analysis makes the solution of social problems a matter of more information rather than more thought—of more surveys, questionnaires, hearings, etc, so that everyone can know what the sources and 'factors' of disputes are. Easton is apparently aware how much of all this is non-action, mere talk, for he expresses the hope that in future there will be more action. This is what most people today are crying for: they want more 'dialogue' and action—not more thinking and analysis.

Inherent in this non-rationalistic attitude is basic conservatism. Although Easton recognizes the existence of the conservative element in behaviouralism, he does not assess precisely the nature of behaviouralist conservatism. Since Burke, conservatives have felt that their society does not need rational analysis: they have assumed that—like the eighteenth-century universe—it is working and will continue to do so if we avoid dangerous experimentations with it. This was a sound enough standpoint from which to answer those who advocated radical changes and revolutions as a solution to what ultimately will seem trivial problems. Revolutions succeed only when they do not succeed—when they fail to destroy the basic order that enables men to live together. But the shift to ideologically-based political orders which began in the eighteenth century has made it imperative to question the non-rational tenets of conservativism. Ideologies are by intent rational orders and raise problems that can only be solved rationally. Because behaviouralism prevents us from doing this, it is 'conservative' in an inappropriate way. That many behaviouralists are in regard to other matters ideological liberals does not change the fact that they are conservative in the worst sense: they are non-rational in their approach to social problems.

Is Post-Behaviouralism Possible?

There are curious references to behaviouralist 'commitment' in Easton's statement: he acknowledges—even charges—that behaviouralists have always been committed to sets of norms which are not an accepted part of behaviouralism. If many critics have commented on the normativist assumptions and consequences of behaviouralism, they have seldom attacked the latter for ivory-towerism. (This charge is more often directed against the traditional political theorist.) Perhaps Easton's emphasis on commitment can be linked with the problem of lack of creative speculation—often considered the main objection to behaviouralist studies. Because of the strict, self-imposed empirical limitations in behavioural studies, no theory—except as a generalized description—has ever resulted. It is possible, however—though he makes no explicit suggestion himself—that Easton believes that commitment and a frank recognition of its rôle will lead to the creative speculation which lies at the roots of genuine theory. (If the reader does not make such a link, it is difficult to understand why Easton should speak of 'post-behaviouralism'.)

Reasoning intended to establish a link between 'commitment' and speculative theorizing might be as follows: all theory requires certain assumptions about the 'nature' of what is being studied, the 'nature' being something more than what is observed. Although in human behaviour these assumptions are variables rather than constants, in order to build a theory we need to treat them as constants; otherwise we would occupy ourselves with transitory phenomena with which behaviouralists are already occupied. Just as the physical scientist will not devote himself to the study of anything so inconstant as the number of fleas on dogs, so a social scientist will not bother with fleeting desires or attitudes. He must believe that what he studies has some degree of permanence before he decides whether it has any 'importance'. The only way to do this is to commit oneself to the norm or norms being studied: to believe that a norm is a constant *is* to commit oneself to it. The problem of 'objectivity' arises only when the commitment is to a normative system or ideology. Normative commitment in the social sciences is only commitment to a belief about the nature of the norm—the degree of its permanence—and parallels the physical scientist's commitment to a belief in the permanence of some of his recorded data.

The difficulty with advocating 'creative speculation' in science is that it is very similar to an ethical appeal to live a good life. While to a normative system creative speculation is an intrinsic good, strict empiricists exclude all speculation: for them empiricism yields not only descriptions, but also generalizations, explanations, and theories themselves. The difference between the empiricists and others is the question of the rôle to be played by creative speculation: we may therefore see in Easton's (implicit) call for this speculation a belief that behaviouralism suffers from the limitations imposed by empirical methodology but that it can be superseded by a new methodology which goes beyond narrow empiricism.

The question is: Can behaviouralism evolve a new methodology, or must the behaviouralist entirely abandon his position and return to traditional political theorizing? The problem with respect to creative speculation has always been how to attach it to our body of knowledge and how to keep it from being mere 'idle speculation'. This has always troubled the empiricist school, of which behaviouralism is a branch. Even when the behaviouralist comes to recognize that empiricism has serious limitations, he has no ready way of integrating speculation with methodology. He may feel that—like anyone else—he can theorize about the nature of empirical phenomena and then test his theory by empirical methodology; however, his problem is that in theory he must make an infinite number of observations; if he attempts to test theory, he will find he has to develop an infinite number of theories. But in effect, he would be doing precisely what he is doing now, because the selection of phenomena for observation is undirected speculation: at least some subconscious theory is present in the process of selection.

The theorist is in a different position. His speculations on human behaviour are limited by his initial assumption that such behaviour follows normative patterns which have 'rational' bounds. Creative speculation has meaning to him because he believes that though men could display an infinite variety of behaviour, they in fact limit it in a way which—given certain elements in the normative pattern—is predictable. He also believes that men limit their normative patterns not because they have been socialized to do so but because the patterns have an explicit meaning to them as human beings and members of a society. This view—which comes close to the theory of natural law—is, of course, bound to upset behaviouralists. Until one produces a convincing argument, supported by empirical evidence that human behaviour is best understood as normative behaviour—having the characteristic of norms attributed before the rise of relativism—it is unlikely that there will be any 'post-behaviouralist' movement which will incorporate anything called 'creative speculation'.

Normativism, Relevance and Rationalism

What has emerged from the conflict between political theory and behaviouralism in the 'post-behavioural era' is a newly-voiced argument for restoring the concept of natural law.[12]

[12] Such is essentially the message of Bruce E Wright's article 'Normative Principles and Prescription in Political Theory', *Bucknell Review*, XIX, No 2 (Fall, 1971), pp 3–36.

What are the prospects and conditions for re-establishing this concept as a measure of reconciliation at a time when the great bulk of political scientists are attempting to analyse political behaviour as if man lacked norms and his behaviour were determined solely by circumstances? If norms are simply generalized descriptions of behaviour, or if they are merely ephemeral desires and attitudes of no more importance than the more specific types of behaviour; if, in other words, the relativist view of norms is correct, then the behaviouralist position is likely to appear valid and the theorist's attempts to analyse political norms seem of little use. Under such circumstances, ideologies are aspects of human behaviour whose 'real' nature will eventually be revealed by behaviouralist studies of specific details of political behaviour and their analysis of the 'true' factors involved. In that event, a defence of political theory requires that the relativist interpretation of norms be proved incorrect.

For theory to be a meaningful activity, norms must be shown as goals actually sought by men and they must form 'logical' (internally consistent) patterns. This requirement is the requirement of relevance and constitutes a distinction between political theory and ethics. Ethics cannot disregard the problem of 'the Good' if it is to remain a philosophical study. Conversely, the political theorist cannot pretend that the norms he deals with are 'the Good' and still remain a political theorist: insofar as he becomes a relativist and argues that the norms of the society he is studying represent 'the Good', he is going beyond the limits of his discipline in its traditional sense.

Political theory has always had close ties with ethics. We can argue in fact that the inability of behaviouralists and theorists to make much use of each other's work reflects to some extent the resistance of the advocates of natural law to philosophic relativism. Behaviouralists apply the principles of relativism to the study of political behaviour and theorists oppose this on what are quite clearly implicit 'natural law' grounds: the behaviouralists, they say, neglect the 'problems' of their society and, by their relativism, become advocates of the existing establishment and its views. Although there is a good deal of truth in this last charge, a solution to the problem of cooperation cannot be found in an automatic return to 'natural law'.

What part can a proposal for a renewed study of natural law play? It does not seem that it can bring about a reconciliation between behaviouralists and theorists. The behaviouralists, as such, have rejected not only the norms of natural law but the rational element in normative behaviour which is an essential assumption for political theory. At this stage the main issue is not natural law versus relativism, but rationally-directed behaviour versus historical, social and biological determinism. What is necessary is a convincing argument for, or a refutation of, the idea that man can and does make genuine choices and that these choices are guided by what we call 'reason'.

The philosophic position with regard to the rational element in normative behaviour requires empirical support, but the difficulty is that the behaviouralists have already committed themselves to the view that human behaviour does not differ in kind from that of any other phenomenon. Behaviouralism and scientism are very closely linked philosophically. What hampers the *rapprochement* of behaviouralism and theory is an unacknowledged normative commitment on the part of behaviouralists. Behaviouralists do not investigate normative sets as logically consistent or inconsistent patterns because they do not believe such patterns exist; furthermore, they are so convinced of the soundness of their view that they do not regard the theorist's counterview as worthy of refutation. If this hindrance to the parallel development of theory and behaviouralism is to be removed, it is essential that in future political theorists offer more evidence in support of their normative position. Behaviouralists have often argued that the bulk of modern theory is a form of exegesis of classical texts. A behaviouralist would furthermore say that there is no point in attempting to produce a definitive reconciliation between, for instance, the claims of individualism and equality, if the ordinary members of society are not trying to do the same on their own level; only if they were, would such theorizing be 'relevant'.

We are not living in the kind of society—and few theorists advocate that kind of society—in which the views of a class of experts can be imposed on the community. In a democracy, the theorist cannot proceed as if he were updating Plato's *Republic*. Does this mean that the theorist has to lapse into relativism? It could be said perhaps that the above is an argument admonishing political theory to make itself more 'relevant' and foster a reconciliation with behaviouralism by accepting at least part of the behavioural viewpoint: that norms as facts of human behaviour and not norms as supposed eternal truths are the immediate concern in a democratic society. But if theory is likely to be made more relevant by this shift of focus, it will not have to be made relativistic, unless it is further assumed that the norms of the individual, the majority, the law, the 'establishment', etc represent 'the Good'. For it is the theorist who understands the irreconcilable conflict such decisions about 'the Good' produce when measured against the theory of democracy; these decisions eliminate one or more of the democratic norms and help promote anti-democratic thinking—fascist, anarchist or communist. At least some features of the latter 'isms' are kept alive in democratic societies today by men who regard themselves as objective researchers in the field of social sciences and do not understand that relativism is not ethically neutral and cannot be so. By arguing (or rather assuming) that norms lack a rational element capable of removing them from the sphere of historical determinism and individual experience, by arguing that there cannot be 'better' norms, the relativist confines himself to those present in the area of his studies (which limit him to a particular time and a particular setting) —unless he has already committed himself to others. Neutrality and objectivity require a rational view of norms.

Postscript: Spragens' Postbehavioural Dilemma

'The dichotomous model of political theory', says T A Spragens, 'has placed the concepts of empirical, descriptive and objective on one side of the divide and the concepts of normative, prescriptive and subjective on the other side. The new paradigm of a reintegrated political theory involves the systematic repudiation of this categorization.'[13] Has Spragens succeeded in reaching his object—'the new paradigm of a reintegrated political theory'? One can agree with his statement that 'political theory cannot be neatly bifurcated into "normative" and "empirical", that no description is wholly "neutral" or unstructured by interpretative canons of order and that norms perform descriptive functions.'[14] But how are we to move 'norms', which modern philosophic analysis has shown to be utterly subjective, to the 'objective' side of the 'bifurcation'? Will it help if we show, as Spragens does, that there are subjective elements in some fundamental assumptions of science? The answer is negative, for it is a fallacy to treat things as identical because they have certain common elements. What we need to know is whether norms are objectively 'descriptive' and whether the findings can give satisfactory answers to Spragens' questions about the objectivity of science.

Behaviouralists usually have no objection to 'norms' as long as they remain objective descriptions. They are not likely for instance to deny the validity of a property norm that receives legal definition and provides the explanation of such concepts as theft, gift and generosity. A large number of today's norms derive from empirical observation rather than traditional ethical and religious injunctions. Consequently, aggression and aggressiveness are modern concepts—with links to psychology and sociology—having little connection with the Christian sin of anger and Christian advocacy of peace and passivity. The main thrust of the social sciences has been to replace the vague prescriptions of traditional ethics with accurate descriptions of how people actually behave and to use the latter as norms.

But a norm of this kind bears little resemblance to what has customarily been called a norm. The 'is' of objectivity cannot logically be the 'ought' of normativity. A description can only be about an 'is': the moment an 'ought' enters, it ceases to be a description. Furthermore, when a norm is treated as a description, as something that 'is', the teleological element is lost: such

---

[13] Thomas A Spragens, Jr, *The Dilemma of Contemporary Political Theory: Toward a Postbehavioral Science of Politics* (Dunellen, New York, 1973), p 117.
[14] *Ibid*, p viii.

an ideal as democracy, for instance, becomes merely a description of states calling themselves 'democracies'.

Spragens is rather obscure on this crucial issue. He includes in the concept of 'description' that of 'norms of fulfillment': 'A final aspect of the descriptive functions of norms worth mentioning is their utility within the context of explanation. Norms may serve an important explanatory role when they are norms of potentiality. That is, certain events in nature or politics may require recourse to norms of fulfillment if their causes are to be intelligible.' He argues further that 'reference to norms of potentiality has been considered illicit by objectivism, in part because such an explanatory form was badly abused by the Aristotelian-based philosophies' but that 'rejection of all such explanations leaves some explanatory lacunae that are impossible to fill by other means.'[15]

What are these lacunae? According to Spragens, 'the [Aristotelian] concept of final cause served to explain the rather common fact of experience that biological developments do seem to have a kind of destination. Similarly, it expressed the widely experienced truth that most human action seems to be guided by some end or purpose.'[16]

What was the abuse by the Aristotelian-based philosophies and how will Spragens remedy it? The following passage seems to provide an answer: 'The application of explanation by final causes to the behaviour of inanimate objects . . . was a misapplication of the principle . . . the absurdities engendered . . . led the protagonists of the seventeenth-century intellectual revolution to reject the whole idea of teleology. What is absurd in the context of physical motion is not so absurd in the context of human action, however.'[17] The key idea on which his argument rests is in the last sentence. What does Spragens mean by 'not so absurd'? Is he willing to see it as 'somewhat absurd' and, if so, what shall be its status in science? Because of the serious objections that have been raised against teleology, if we are trying to reintegrate teleology into philosophic and

[15] *Ibid*, p 127.
[16] *Ibid*, p 45.
[17] *Ibid*, p 133.

scientific thinking, we should unequivocally state our purpose. Issues cannot be clarified otherwise. Behaviouralists are not likely to change their methodology until it can be shown that norms—which Spragens clearly regards as supplying the order[18]—can be defended as descriptions in which the teleological element has a logical justification. But he has not attempted to do this in any systematic way.

[18] See his references to norms as 'criteria or standards of order' (p 119); 'ordering patterns' (p 123) etc.

Index

Arendt, Hannah, 47n., 50n.
Aristotle, 31, 71, 71n.; concept of final cause of, 168
Authority: and choice, 57–8; crisis of, 47–9; and government, 60; de Jouvenel on, 49–54; misconception of, 63–4; nature of, 56n.; and political obligation, 59–60; and relativism, 65–6; and society v. individual, 59–60; and sovereignty, 61–8, 82–4, 93; Winch on, 54–9
Ayer, Alfred Jules, 96n.; on ethical and tautological statements, 96

Barker, Sir Ernest, 11n., 12, 13, 35n., 36
Barry, Brian, 38n.; on public interest, 38–41; on Rousseau, 39, 41
Behaviouralism: on authority, 84–5; Easton on, 159–61; and legitimacy, 87–8; nature of, 14; and new methodology, 162–3; and norms, 167, 169; and philosophy, 156–8; and political theory, 2, 165–6; and scientism, 145, 165
Bentham, Jeremy: on public interest, 33
Between Past and Future (H. Arendt), 47n.

Bodenheimer, Edgar, 33, 34n.
Bodin, Jean, 71, 75n., 77; on sovereignty, 72–3, 75, 76
Brecht, Arnold, 134n.; on scientific-value relativism, 133–4
Burke, Edmund, 160

Carnap, R., 96
Carritt, E. F., 27n., 28
Church, 26, 123, 143; and science, 145–7; and state, 106n., 143
Civility, 125
Cobban, Alfred, 29n.
Constitutionalism, 11, 12, 13, 14, 18
Contemporary Political Science: Toward Empirical Theory (I. de Sola Pool), 14n.
Courier, Paul Louis, 9n.

Democracy: and authority, 64–5; and the General Will, 28; and individualism, 8–11, 36–7; and individualism and egalitarianism, 46; and natural law, 111–13, 117, 123–5; and post-behaviouralism, 167–8; and Public Interest, 34–5, 44–5; and sovereignty, 34, 78, 83; and welfare, 42–3; and values, 124–5
D'Entrèves, A. P., 116, 116n.

171

Dicey, A. V., 71
Dilemma of Contemporary Political Theory: Toward a Postbehavioral Science of Politics, The (Thomas A. Spragens), 167n.

Easton, David, 158n.; on behaviouralism, 159–61; on commitment, 161–2
Edel, Abraham, 128n.
Egalitarianism: Egalitarian theory and state, 51; and General Will, 31; and individualism, 15–19; as norm in democracy, 111; and sovereignty, 51, 77–8; and welfare, 42–3 (*see also* Equality)
Einstein, Albert, 135
Empiricism: and game playing, 154–5; limitations of, 151–2; and normativism, 149; and physical sciences, 149–50; and political theory, 153–4; and relativism, 152–3; in social sciences, 147–9, 151–2
Equality, 15, 117; literal, 77; and public interest, 42 (*see also* Egalitarianism)
Essays in the Public Philosophy (W. Lippmann), 126n.
Ethical and Political Thinking (E. F. Carritt), 27n.
Ethical Judgment (A. Edel), 128n.
Eulau, Heinz, 14n.

Faure, Edgar, 7n.
Freedom: and free will, 53; relativists' view of, 142; Winch and freedom of choice, 57–9

Galileo, G., 147
Games and Decisions (Luce and Raiffa), 21

Games Theory, 22; game playing, 154–5
General Will: Barker on, 35–6; Barry on, 39–41; and democracy, 30–33; and games theory, 22; and Public Interest, 25ff.; and Rousseau, 25–6, 28–33; and totalitarianism, 26–30
Goedel, K., 100
Gough, J. W., 12n., 13
Government: contractual government, 23–4; democratic, 37, 38–9; and legitimacy, 88–9; and natural law, 116–17; nature of, 116; and priorities, 139; and public interest, 33–4, 41; and relativism, 110; representative government, 22–3; and sovereignty, 80–81

Hall, Everett W., 16, 17n.
Hegel, Friedrich, 30
Heraclitus, 133n.
Hinsley, F. H., 76n.; on sovereignty, 76
Hobbes, Thomas, 3, 4, 21, 36, 38, 71, 75n., 77, 90, 111, 126, 141; on authority, 61–2; and de Jouvenel, 51–2; on human behaviour, 80; and natural law, 140, 141; and political theory, 143; and relativism, 140–43; on sovereignty, 73–4, 75, 76
Hume, David, 71
Hunter, J. F. M., 19n., 20

In Defense of Sovereignty (W. J. Stankiewicz, ed.), 1, 72n., 77n.
Individualism: and democracy, 36–7; and human nature, 36; in modern society, 13–17; as

norm in democracy, 111; and relativism, 98–9; and Social Contract, 21–3; as a value, 8ff.
Introduction to Equity, An (G. W. Keeton), 121n.
Intuitionism, 18n.

Jouvenel, Bertrand de, 48n., 50n., 52n., 55n., 57; on authority, 49–50, 52–3; and Hobbes, 51–2

Keeton, G. W., 121n.
Kelsen, Hans, 45, 62

Language, Truth and Logic (A. J. Ayer), 96n.
Laski, Harold, 71, 72
Ledru-Rollin, Alexandre Auguste, 52
Legitimacy, 82; concept of, 87–8; of government, 65–6; of laws, 113; and sovereignty, 88–90
Leviathan (T. Hobbes), 75n.
Lindsay, A. D., 32n.
Lippmann, Walter, 126n.; on public philosophy, 125–6
Lipset, S. M., 87n., 88; on legitimacy, 87
Luce, Robert Duncan, 21

Machiavelli, Niccolo, 47n.
Marx, Karl, 30
Masks of Society, The (John F. A. Taylor), 17n.
Modern Democratic State, The (A. D. Lindsay), 32n.

Natural Law: Cobban on, 29; determination of, 104–7; and democracy, 123–5, 111–13; and ethics, 99, 118–19; and ideology, 111–12; new arguments for, 163–5; and norms, 107–9; and positive law, 109–15, 119–22; and post-behavioural era, 163–6; and public philosophy, 125–7; and 'reasonableness in action,' 116–17; and relativism, 99; and relativists, 110–13, 124–5
Natural Law (A. P. d'Entrèves), 116n.
Nomos V: The Public Interest, 34n.
Nomos X: Representation, 14n.
Normativism, 148, 163ff.; attitude to 'inconsistencies', 153; and empiricism, 149
Norms: and authority, 52–3; behaviouralists on, 167–8; and empiricism, 14; and free will, 53; interpretations of, 108–9; and leadership, 52–4; natural law norms, 115–16; and public interest, 44; and relativism, 45, 102, 130–33, 136, 152–3; as 'restrictions', 105–6; 'supreme' norm, 45–6; as tools of analysis, 131–3

Peters, R. S., 55
Philosophy of Democratic Government (Yves R. Simon), 9n.
Plato, 30, 105, 165
Political Man (F. M. Lipset), 87n.
Political obligation, 19ff.; misunderstanding of, 60–61; and natural law, 118–19; and positive law, 63–4, 117–19; and relativist society, 59
Political Philosophy (A. Quinton, ed.), 38n., 54n.
Political Theory: The Foundations of Twentieth-Century Political Thought (A. Brecht), 134n.
Politics, The (Aristotle), 71
Pool, Ithiel de Sola, 14n.

Positive Law: and ethics, 119–22; and natural law, 109–15, 119–22; and values, 122

Post-behaviouralism: Easton on, 161–2; and natural law, 163–6; and norms, 168–9; and 'speculation', 162–3; Spragens on, 166–9

Pour un nouveau contrat social (E. Faure), 7n.

Principles of Social and Political Theory (E. Barker), 35n.

Prisoner's dilemma, 20–4

Public Interest: concept of public interest norms, 41; and democratic norms, 44–6; and General Will, 25ff.; nature of, 33–7; and public assistance, 42–3; and Rousseau's General Will, 25–7; and sovereignty, 34–5, 79–81

Public Philosophy: Lippmann on, 125–6; and natural law, 125–6; and sovereignty, 126–7

Quinton, Anthony, 38

Raiffa, Howard, 21

Rawls, John, 16, 17, 17n., 18, 18n., 19

Relativism: and authority, 65–6; Brecht on, 134; consequences of, 157–8; and democracy, 124–5;
and empiricism, 152–3; and freedom, 117, 142; and government, 110; and Hobbes, 140–42; as methodology, 134–5, 141–3; and natural law, 99–102, 110–13; nature of, 129–31, 133, 135; and norms, 45, 60, 102–4, 131–33, 152–3; and objectivity, 146–7; and obligation, 59–61; and priorities of government, 139; and relativity, 137; scientific value relativism, 133–4; and scientism, 145; and sovereignty, 94–5; and study of society, 137–9; types of, 128; and values, 97–9, 100, 101, 139–43

Republic, The (Plato), 97, 105, 165

Rousseau, Jean Jacques, 31n., 34, 37, 71; Barry on, 39, 41, and communism, 28–30; and General Will, 25–6, 28–33

Rousseau and the Modern State (A. Cobban), 29n.

Runciman, W. G., 21n., 22

Russell, Bertrand, 96

Sartori, Giovanni, 14n.

Science: and Church, 145–7; and philosophy, 155–6; social science and philosophy, 156–7

Scientism, 1, 3; and behaviouralism, 145, 156–7; scientific method and relativism, 130–1, 134; and theory, 144

Sen, Amartya K., 21n., 22

Simon, Yves R., 9n.

Six Books of the Commonweale, The (J. Bodin), 75n.

Social Contract: fate of, 7; and government, 23–4; Hunter on, 19–21; individualism and the contract theory, 12–17; and justice, 17–19; and the 'Prisoner's dilemma', 21–4; its two sets of values, 8–11

Social Contract: Essays by Locke, Hume, and Rousseau (E. Barker), 11n., 35n.

Social Contract, The (J. W. Gough), 12n.

Social Contract, The (J. J. Rousseau), 31n.

Social Sciences: empirical approach in, 147–53; and norms, 131–3; and objectivity, 146–7; and philosophy, 156
Sovereignty: and authority, 48–9, 62–3, 66–8, 82–4, 93; and balance of power, 93–4; classical theory of, 51; conflicting concepts of, 86; and crisis of authority, 47ff; and democracy, 82–3; definition of, 76–7; dilemma of, 74–5; and egalitarianism, 77–8; and government, 80–82; Hobbesian, 69–70, 73–4; and international law, 90–92; and law and order, 79–80; and legitimacy, 87–90; locus of, 71–2; meaning of, 69; misconception of, 64; and political analysts, 84–5; and public philosophy, 126–7; and relativism, 94–5; restatement of (W. J. Stankiewicz), 76; types of, 69n.
Sovereignty (F. H. Hinsley), 76n.
Sovereignty: An Inquiry into the Political Good (B. de Jouvenel), 48n., 50n.
Spencer, Herbert, 12
Spragens, T. A., Jr., 167n.; on political theory, 166–9
State, 82, 144; and Church, 106n., 143; Hegelian, 59, 116, and private conscience, 63

Taylor, John F. A., 16, 17n.
Theory of Justice, A (J. Rawls), 17n.
Thrasymachus, 97, 129
Totalitarianism, 27, 28, 34; and General Will, 27–30
Tucker, A. W., 21

Utilitarianism, 33, 111, 136

Weber, Max, 67
Winch, Peter, 54n.; on authority, 54–9
Wittgenstein, Ludwig, 57, 96
Wright, Bruce E., 163n.